Sherwood Anderson

Sherwood Anderson

Irving Howe

Stanford University Press
Stanford, California

To My Father

Part of the chapter " 'A Will to Splendor' " originally appeared in *Commentary* under the title "Sherwood Anderson and the Power Urge," Copyright 1950 by *Commentary*. The chapter "The Book of the Grotesque" originally appeared in *Partisan Review*, Copyright 1951 by *Partisan Review*. Part of the chapter "Conditions of Fame" originally appeared in *Tomorrow* under the title "Sherwood Anderson and the American Myth of Power," Copyright 1949 by Garrett Publications, Inc. The chapter "In the Lawrencian Orbit" originally appeared in *Furioso* under the title "Sherwood Anderson and D. H. Lawrence," Copyright 1950 by Reed Whittemore.

Contents

Author's Note, 1966

I T IS hard to be a minor writer—hard perhaps in any country, but especially in the United States. Visions of the grandiose sweep through our national imagination. We improvise greater writers each decade, naïvely supposing that our will or enthusiasm, and sometimes nothing more than our publicity, can do for us what only time has done for Europe. It seems to us—though heaven alone knows why!—that we deserve great writers, perhaps on the same principle that we have big cities, large budgets, immense buildings, and tall tales.

Now as it happens, we have had a rather impressive number of great or near-great writers in America: Melville, Twain, James, Faulkner, Eliot, and Stevens. But this list, or another like it, is not really calculated to satisfy the inflated appetites our culture has developed for self-congratulation and self-aggrandizement. The result is that a few of our writers are systematically overpraised, while others, more modest in achievement, are badly neglected. For what has been distinctive in American literature is a tradition of gifted figures who managed only once or twice to realize their talent. One thinks of Howells in some of his comic novels; or Sarah Orne Jewett in a few exquisite stories; or Harold Frederic in a single remarkable novel; or Sherwood Anderson in a group of short fictions. But in our mania for the grand, we brush past the fine.

Sherwood Anderson was a minor writer, though in a few crucial instances he did first-rate, perhaps even major, work. He was a minor writer, yet one who ought to be of special interest to Americans, for in his stories he evoked aspects of our experience—those feelings of loneliness, yearning, and muted love—which lie buried beneath the surface of our culture.

When my book on Anderson first appeared, it was attacked by those who could not bear him and by those who could not bear to have him criticized. That was quite as it should have been, for it seems to me entirely right that both groups of readers and critics should have found the book, or parts of it, distressing. It could not satisfy those who looked upon Anderson as a linsey-woolsey D. H. Lawrence, a prophet risen in the provinces; it could not satisfy those who saw him merely as a soft-headed sentimentalist. That I found myself somewhere between these embattled opinions—or as I prefer to think, apart from the excesses of both—is not of course an automatic warrant of virtue and perception. It is possible, after all, that either the partisans or opponents of Anderson are right, and I was wrong.

But upon returning to this book after a long absence, and in going through Anderson's work again, I find to my pleasure that I can stand by the judgments I made fifteen years ago. Anderson never wrote a completely satisfying novel, despite the excellence of a section here, a chapter there; he was often a self-indulgent writer and a murky thinker; and the public stance he sometimes affected, as the vulnerable and self-conscious artist, strikes me as largely tiresome. But in his masterpiece, *Winesburg, Ohio*, as in a half-dozen stories and the first part of *Poor White*, he wrote with a purity of voice, a loveliness of tact, a sweetness of compassion, such as few Americans have ever reached. "The Egg" seems to me one of the greatest stories ever written, a masterpiece of grotesque pathos that will live as long as the English language survives. Is that not enough, then, for an American writer — and especially for a man like Anderson, whose struggle to escape the constrictions of his youth and the dullness of his young manhood, whose lifelong groping toward articulation and grace, make him seem an almost "mythic" American figure?

Reading through this book again, I find myself wishing — quite in the manner of Anderson's own characters — that I could have a second chance at it. I should like to ease and chasten the prose. I should like to absorb a little more gracefully than I did the psychological speculations which a figure like Anderson seems to enforce. And I should like to say to the younger self who wrote this book, the intimate stranger bearing my name, that in a full-scale work it is not really necessary to try to make every sentence stern with discrimination, tense with response.

But there is no second chance. The book must stand as it was written, with its evident faults and possible virtues. As it goes into this new printing, I hope that it will help a new generation of readers discover the haunting beauty of Sherwood Anderson's stories.

I. H.

June 1, 1966

Preface

THIS book is partly an outgrowth of an involved and intimate relationship I have had with Sherwood Anderson's writings, a relationship I believe not unique to myself. When I read *Winesburg, Ohio* in my adolescence, I felt that a new world had been opened to me, new possibilities of experience, new dimensions of emotion. Not many years later I found myself rejecting Anderson's work: I was impatient with his vagueness, superior to his uncertainty. Yet he still meant more to me than other writers of unquestionably greater achievement.

One Sunday in 1943 I was hitchhiking through Ohio; it was my last week end before sailing overseas with the army. I remember with an undiminished sense of exhilaration a journey I took along a side road that led to Clyde, Anderson's home town and model for *Winesburg*. As I should have anticipated, Clyde looked much like other American small towns and the few of its people with whom I talked were not particularly interested in Sherwood Anderson. But my pilgrimage nonetheless gave me a sense of satisfaction I could hardly have explained.

Now, in this book, I hope to achieve a synthesis of feeling and opinion toward Anderson's work. The original awe that I, like so many others, felt upon reading *Winesburg* it would be impossible to recapture. The later impatience with some of his books it would be erroneous to repudiate. But I have come to believe that while much of his work remains unacceptable there is nonetheless a precious remnant particularly valuable to our day and situation. And without evading the task of rejecting where rejection is due, I hope that from this book there may emerge a clear statement of those values in Anderson's work which are worthy of our admiration.

In preparing this book I have consulted those of Anderson's relatives, friends, and literary associates whom I could reach and who were willing to make available their recollections. Much of the biographical material derives from these interviews and I gratefully acknowledge the aid of the following: Karl Anderson, Trigant Burrow, Elliot Cohen, Loretta Cooper, Saxe Cummins, George Daugherty, Mitchell Dawson, John Emerson, William Faulkner, James Fiebleman, Waldo Frank, Julius Friend, Ben Huebsch, Edna Kenton, Manuel Komroff, Anita Loos, Margaret Marshall, Max Radin, Ferdinand Schevill, Roger Sergel, Max Wald, Edmund Wilson, Stanley Young.

I must particularly mention the help given me by Mrs. Eleanor Anderson who supplied material about her deceased husband without hesitation, despite the fact that we both knew she could hardly sympathize with some of my aims in this book.

I have had stimulating conversations with a number of Anderson's critics: Waldo Frank, Horace Gregory, and Lionel Trilling. The help and encouragement I have received from Lionel Trilling form only one of my debts to him. And to Leslie Fiedler I am indebted for bringing to my attention a point in Anderson's work that has been generally ignored.

The staff of the Newberry Library, which cares for a large collection of Anderson material, has been of inestimable service to me and I hereby extend my gratitude to Amy Nyholm, Gertrude Woodward, and Charlotte Dobbs. Much of the biographical material in the first two chapters comes from excellent Ph.D. studies by William Sutton and William Phillips, cited in the bibliography. Sections of the book have been read and helpfully criticised by Alfred Kazin, Richard Hofstadter, and David Sachs. The close reading by David Sachs is the kind of service one can expect only from a devoted friend.

Since I do not know how to express adequately my debt to my wife, I merely acknowledge it here in the hope that she will accept the gratitude I owe her in so many ways and for so many reasons.

Portions of this book have appeared in *Commentary, Furioso, Kenyon Review, Partisan Review,* and *Tomorrow.* These magazine versions were early drafts, and in several instances have been considerably rewritten for their final form in this book. I wish to thank Roger Sergel for a persuasive communication suggesting several changes.

It remains only to be said that none of the people who have helped me are responsible for what I have written.

I. H.

[1951]

Acknowledgments

THE author wishes to thank Creative Age Press for permission to quote from *Paul Rosenfeld, Voyager of the Arts*, edited by Jerome Mellquist and Lucie Wiese; *The Saturday Review of Literature* for permission to quote from "My Brother, Sherwood Anderson," by Karl Anderson; Rinehart & Company for permission to quote from *Across Spoon River*, by Edgar Lee Masters; The Newberry Library for permission to quote from various articles in its special Sherwood Anderson *Bulletin*; Random House for permission to quote from *The Autobiography of Alice B. Toklas* by Gertrude Stein; Liveright Publishing Corporation for permission to quote from *Dark Laughter, A New Testament, Hello Towns!, Perhaps Women,* and *Death in the Woods*; Viking Press for permission to quote from *Winesburg, Ohio* and *Mid-American Chants*; and Mrs. Eleanor Anderson for permission to quote from those writings of Sherwood Anderson to which she holds the copyright and from his letters stored at the Newberry Library.

Sherwood Anderson

"A Fair and Sweet Town"

IN THE economy of late-19th-century America, Ohio was unique among the states. Like the eastern seaboard it was seized by a passion for finance; in its cities massive industries sprang up, and from Cleveland the Rockefeller group began to dominate American business. At the same time, however, the frontier atmosphere of social novelty and "roominess" had not yet completely evaporated from its life. Ohio stood midway on the scale of social organization between the commercial East and the agrarian West, subject to the blunt pressures and tacit influences of both, yet socially distinct from either.

Most of the significant impulses in American society could be found in the Ohio of the 1880's. The state was no longer on the frontier, its usable land having been largely occupied by 1850 and thousands of its own people having since moved westward; but echoes of the frontier, of its mores and its social tone, still hung over the villages and small towns. Something yet remained, if only an intimate memory, of what now seems the most attractive historical moment in American life: that egalitarian interval bounded on the one side by Jacksonian democracy and on the other by the Civil War. In the small towns there could still be found fluid relationships among levels of the population not quite hardened into classes. On the farms the system of small owning was firmly established; by 1880 there were a quarter of a million individually owned farms in Ohio, averaging some 90 acres each and in their vast majority worked by the men who owned them. So unsentimental an observer of the American scene as James Bryce could write in the late 1880's:

> Contrast any of these countries [in Europe] with the United States, where the working classes are as well fed, clothed and lodged as the lower middle-classes in Europe, and the farmers who till their own land (as nearly all do) much better, where a good education is within the reach of the poorest, where the opportunities for getting on in one way or another are so abundant. . . . Pauperism already exists and increases in some of the larger cities. . . . But outside these few cities one sees nothing but comfort. . . . All over the wide West from Lake Ontario to the Upper Missouri, one travels past farms of two to three hundred acres, in every one of which there is a spacious farmhouse among orchards and meadows, where the farmer's children grow up strong and hearty on abundant food. . . . It is impossible not to feel warmed, cheered, invigorated by the sense of such material well-being all around one, impossible not to be infected by the buoyancy and hopefulness of the people.

If this description be viewed in terms of the country's historical development rather than its condition at the time Bryce wrote, the crucial sentence would be, "Pauperism already exists and increases in some of the larger cities." As early as 1850 Ohio, though still basically agricultural, was fourth among the states as producer of manufactured goods. In the next 30 years Cleveland and Akron grew wildly; the cities, pressed by new factories, began to generate tenements and crimes, slums and *lumpenproletarians.*

The central fact about Ohio life in the late 19th century is thus the temporary coexistence of sharply contrasting types of social organization. It is precisely this conjunction which has been neglected by those historians who tend to view the frontier and the recent frontier as isolated historical sectors moving autonomously to more advanced stages of economy. The Turner thesis, as the historian Richard Hofstadter has written, envisaged an "American evolution [that] had been a repeated return to primitive conditions on a continually receding frontier line, a constant repetition of development from simple conditions to a complex society." Absent from Turner's theory of American historical development was an awareness of the "law of combined development"—the "law" that a primitive society contiguous with an advanced one will not laboriously and schematically repeat all of the latter's stages of growth but will rather telescope them by imposing advanced techniques on its backwardness.

The world in which Sherwood Anderson grew up was not merely western, it was a mixture of all those social atmospheres we call eastern and western, urban and rural, industrial and handicraft. The sharp memory of the frontier or the growing shadow of the city—which was more important? It is a moot question and hardly worth answering, for what was important was their convergence.

There has probably never been another occasion in American history when it was possible to see or to sense the presence of so many conflicting strands of the past and the future, and for the alert witness, be he intellectual or intuitive, this milieu could serve as the foundation for an inclusive view of American experience. Perhaps the most advantageous position for such a witness was neither the city nor the farm, but rather the small town in which people retained the essential rural qualities even as they strained for the urban successes. Such a town was Clyde, in the central north of Ohio.

When Henry Howe, the great Ohio traveler, took his second tour in the 1880's he noted that "Clyde is a wholesome, cleanly appearing town." Its population was never to reach much more than 3,000, and partly because the nearby land was a sandy loam suited for raising cabbages and cultivating berry patches, it was always to remain a farm town. In the early summer Clyde's residents would drop their work for a week or two to go berry-picking, and in the fall Clyde's main streets would be filled with wagons heavy with cabbages. Most of the townspeople were in direct economic relations with the farmers, either selling them goods and services or, less frequently, renting them land.

In the 1880's Clyde was still a young town, some of its residents probably able to remember when it had been founded half a century earlier. In 1816 Jesse Benton had settled at a spring of clear water on Clyde's present site, building a log cabin and claiming 80 acres of land. By 1828 the settlement began to assume the outlines of a town, streets being laid out and the first frame building constructed. Most of the settlers were Yankees in whom there remained strong residues of the New England moral attitudes.

In such a town the memories of early travail, of its own "frontier" were necessarily vivid. A few old men could remember the first appearance of post coaches in 1832. There were still living witnesses of the railroad's first entry in 1852 and the establishing of the first brick business block seven years later. The sense of newness, of being part of a large uncharted national expansion, freshened the town's consciousness.

Though Clyde's residents were mainly of New England descent, some aspects of its life were decidedly unlike anything associated with New England. The weekly *Clyde Enterprise* ran regular appeals for prohibition, but during Sherwood Anderson's boyhood there were as many as 16 saloons in the town. In the winter of 1886 the *Enterprise* reported that within ten minutes eight brawls had broken out at a dance in the Opera House. The actual frontier had passed westward some decades before but its atmosphere lingered—in a burst of violence, a display of social crudity, an hour of public reminiscence.

Physically too, the town betrayed its rawness. In the winter of 1885 the *Enterprise* sadly noted that there is "plenty of mud in Clyde when it rains," and during the same year the paving of streets in Fremont, the county seat, aroused much discussion and envy in Clyde. For Clyde was one of those unfortunate towns that can never quite live up to the image they strive to construct of themselves.

In its dominant values Clyde still accepted the New England heritage. Long after the Puritan tone had curdled in its original setting, it found a new support in the

Midwest, where the harshness of farm and village life made for a certain receptivity to a code of stricture. Each week the *Enterprise* chanted the litany of "uplift," taught its readers the elements of courtesy and manners, and printed moralistic short stories to enrich their spiritual resources. Blending a slightly diluted Calvinism with the jargon of "progress," the paper urged its readers to join the American quest for quick wealth and struck a note of optimism about Clyde's future which the facts hardly justified.

It would be wrong, however, to take too harsh a view of small-town Ohio life during the last decades of the 19th century. There were, to be sure, the social and cultural crudities that followed from an unfelicitous mixture of East and West, but there were also mild graces and spontaneous pleasures. In the social life of a town like Clyde there was often a sense of community that one cannot help finding attractive, no matter how distasteful one also finds the sentimental reminiscences it would later evoke. And large though the drawbacks undoubtedly were, one must also remember that they were at the time usually unavoidable. For as a Clyde historian remarks: "Small pox was still prevalent in 1882; cheap lands were still sold in Kansas by the Union Pacific Railway; polygamy was still practised in Utah." The country was far from "settled."

In the 1880's there were still in Clyde those skilled craftsmen who were to make so deep an impression on Sherwood Anderson and many other writers of his generation. The *Enterprise*, for example, carried advertisements from the Vogt Brothers announcing handsome carriages made entirely in their own shops. But the winds were blow-ing the other way, and Clyde was only too eager to join in what Bryce was to call "the amazing fuss" Americans made over money. A few industries, not snared by the cities, somehow found their way to the town. A small cutlery plant had been operating since 1850, a granite company was established in the 1870's, and a few years later bicycle and sauerkraut factories were opened. But this, of course, was as nothing when compared with the expansion of other Ohio towns. In Anderson's *Memoirs*, written at the end of his life, he has recalled the atmosphere of his boyhood years:

> There was something strange happening to our town that must have been happening at about the same time to thousands of American towns: a sudden and almost universal turning of men from the old handicrafts toward our modern life of the machines. . . .
>
> It meant the end of the old craftsmen of the towns, the shoemakers, the harness, wagon, buggy, furniture and clothing makers. All the little shops scattered through the towns, shops in which men fashioned things with their hands directly out of the raw materials furnished by nature, were to disappear with amazing rapidity . . . It was a kind of fever, an excitement in the veins of the people. . . .

For the merchants of Clyde this excitement was largely vicarious: the orgy of industry-building and money-making barely touched them. In the fall of 1885 the *Enterprise* hopefully announced that "building in Clyde is beginning to boom and business generally is reviving." The natural-gas craze then sweeping Ohio, sometimes with spectacular results, also reached Clyde, and in May 1886 "The Clyde Natural Gas Company" bought a lot for drilling. Bravely the *Enterprise* cheered the venture forward, but a year later it was forced to report, "Gas well set on fire—Derrick burned—Management muffed generally." Nonetheless, the year 1886 seems to have been a high point in Clyde's business life. Three railroads were then passing through the town, several factories were operating, and a branch of the Knights of Labor, with 20 members, was formed. But no fundamental change was to take place in the town's economy, and after a few false spurts Clyde settled back in disappointed recognition that it was forever to remain a drowsy farmers' town.

In this milieu Sherwood Anderson spent his boyhood, here were formed the basic patterns of his character. Without visible irony or malice, Anderson was to remember Clyde in his last years as a "fair and sweet town."

The Anderson family line has been traced to the early years of the 19th century, when Sherwood's great-grandfather, Robert Anderson, moved from Pennsylvania to a 300-acre farm near West Union, a newly founded village in Ohio. With Robert came an 11-year-old son James, who grew up to be a prosperous farmer, admired by his neighbors for his industry, humor, and violent antislavery opinions. The family's calm pastoral rhythm of life was broken by the Civil War when James's 18-year-old son Irwin entered the Union army and saw considerable action in Tennessee. After his army service Irwin attended school for a year and then wandered off to Missouri for four or five years—though about this period of his life nothing is known. When he returned to Ohio in 1871 Irwin Anderson was a handsome young man of 25 or 26 who, perhaps as a reaction to the war or perhaps in response to demands of his own nature, had broken away from his family's pattern of hard-working farm life. But he was not, of course, as his son Sherwood was later to write and as many of Sherwood's critics were to repeat, "a ruined dandy from the South."

Irwin settled in Morning Sun, an Ohio village of 135 people, where he "set up" as a harness maker, a trade he probably learned during his cavalry service. In Morning Sun he seemed a dashing fellow: he could tell lively stories about his war experience, he had traveled west, he was by nature gregarious and ebullient, and he seemed just a bit more gallant than most other young men of the village. In 1872 he met Emma Smith, a good-looking girl who worked as "hired girl" for a local family, and a year later married her.

Emma's family background is almost unknown, and the little that is known has been distorted in the reminiscences of her son Sherwood. In his three autobiographical volumes (*A Story Teller's Story, Tar,* and the *Memoirs*) he pictured Emma's mother as a gusty Italian, "a dark evil old woman with . . . broad hips and . . . great breasts," who had once beaten a thief with her bare fists and then invited him to the back yard for a cider bout. She was actually a prosaic German, prudish, nasty-nice, anything but immoral. In later years this "dark evil old woman" was to berate her son-in-law, Irwin Anderson, for not going to church regularly.

Sherwood was also to weave wistful fantasies into his memories of his mother; in his *Memoirs* he has written that she was a "bound girl" from the age of nine. But the visions of adolescent serfdom suggested by this phrase are quite unwarranted, for Emma had not been "bound" and had actually been well cared for by the family with whom she lived as half-ward and half-servant. A diary kept by Emma as a girl shows an affectionate and intimate relationship between the "bound girl" and her "masters."

By the middle of 1874 the Irwin Andersons had moved to Camden, Ohio, a small town in the southwest of the state where Irwin opened a harness shop. That same year their first child, Karl, was born, and a year later came Stella. On September 3, 1876 Emma Anderson gave birth to her third child, Sherwood.

In Camden the Andersons were liked and respected. "Cap" Anderson (the title was bestowed retrospectively) was known to drink a bit but not excessively, he played the alto horn in the village band and practised in the back of his store during slack hours, and for a short while he even taught Sunday school. Apparently he was more successful with horns than harness, for by about 1880 he moved from Camden to Caledonia, a town in central Ohio. For years the rumor was to linger in Camden that he had fled to escape his leather bills. In the meantime another son, Irving, was born.

As they moved from town to town, the Andersons gradually slid down the gently inclined social scale of agrarian Ohio. In Caledonia "Cap" still had his own shop but apparently began to neglect it; the man from whom he rented it was to remember, 60 years later, that "Cap" was "a great story teller" and "might have gone on a little toot once in a while."

By 1884, shortly after the birth of still another son, Ray, the Andersons moved to Clyde. Once an independent craftsman who had delegated to a helper the unpleasant task of making halters, Irwin Anderson was now reduced to working as a hand in the Ervin Brothers' harness shop. (Perhaps by way of compensation he rose in military status: Clyde knew him as "Major" Anderson.) Within a year he lost his job, partly because of his fondness for "little toots" and partly because, having once been his own master, he now found it hard to work steadily for others.

Most of Sherwood Anderson's recollections of boyhood seem to have been based on the family's experience during one particularly harsh winter, which he was to identify as that of 1886-87 and his boyhood chum, Herman Hurd, as that of 1885-86. Hurd was probably right. In the winter of 1885-86 Emma Anderson was bearing Earl, her last child; Irwin Anderson was working only irregularly; and for the first time the family knew want if not hunger. During most of Sherwood's boyhood, however, the family's poverty was not nearly so extreme as he later described it, nor was his father ever "an outlaw in the community." Irwin Anderson, it is true, was slightly depreciated in Clyde as a garrulous fellow who didn't quite fulfill his family responsibilities, but he was also liked for his convenient joviality and his even more convenient willingness to give his time to community enterprise.

Irwin soon found an occupation which allowed him the freedom of movement he so much needed: he became a sign- and house-painter. For sign jobs, his eldest son, the artistic Karl, would do the lettering and he would fill in the outlines. For houses (so Sherwood later remembered) the father would take along the older boys and tell Civil War stories while they worked—though Karl, in his old age, could not recall having ever gone on such an expedition. In his *Memoirs* Sherwood described this period as one in which

> we had begun to prosper a little. Now father had become a house painter. He had begun to speak a new language. There was much talk of the fine art of mixing house paint, of how the brush should be held in the hand. At that time there was a great passion for what was called "graining". . . . Father had acquired an outfit of graining tools and practised on the doors and walls of our house.

To increase the family income and perhaps also to provide it with a base more stable than did her husband, Emma began to take in washing. "I always remember keenly," Sherwood was to write, "a kind of shame that began to grow in the breasts of us children when we were sent off to bear home baskets of dirty clothes or to return them washed and ironed." But while intermittently difficult, the family's economic condition was seldom desperate. William Sutton, the scholar on whose doctoral study of Anderson's early life all his biographers must lean, has discovered a photograph of the Anderson family, taken in the late 1880's, which shows the children dressed in good clothes—Sunday clothes no doubt but still evidence that there was enough money to have Sunday clothes.

It pleased the wealthier townspeople when the Anderson boys showed an industriousness their father did not. Sherwood, particularly, became a penny-hunting, preternaturally shrewd boy, always on the lookout for a better part-time job, and the businessmen of Clyde thought it good to encourage him, to prod him with talk of "getting on" and applaud his precocious sharpness. Sherwood's younger brother and closest boyhood pal, Irving, was to remember him as a highly aggressive newsboy, and in a memoir Karl Anderson writes that

> Sherwood, the exuberant one, was known as "the go-getter." He wanted to get on in the world. On Saturday afternoons he was on the streets selling the week-end edition of the *Cincinnati Enquirer* . . . to the farmers who came to town to do their own shopping, and he was proud that he could sell more copies of the paper than any other boy in town. Once he boasted of his persuasiveness in inducing a farmer in a bar-room to buy more than one copy of the *Enquirer*.

Though there was not then the faintest foreshadow of his mature literary gifts, the talents that were to make him a first-rate advertising man he already had in abundance—talents which, try as he might, he would never be able to suppress.

By even the most conventional American standards, Sherwood was pre-eminently a normal boy: socially extroverted and highly responsible, neither conspicuously brilliant nor persistently moody. He liked baseball and since he couldn't play well he edged himself into the managership of The Clyde Stars; he liked horses and to be near them he would occasionally work as a swipe, once experiencing the transcendent thrill of carting a horse to Fremont. Because of his inventiveness and energy, he was highly popular among boys of his own age; his closest friends were simple boys, Herman Hurd, who was to follow his father into the grocery business, and Barley Mann, who was to become a barber. On Spring Street, where the Andersons lived before moving to the dilapidated "Piety Hill" section, there can still be found a small cave where Sherwood and his friends signed their names in blood to enter the fraternity of pirates.

But through pressing necessity, and perhaps to compensate for his father's indifference to economic problems, Sherwood quickly moved into the adult world. During his teens he worked as a newsboy, errand boy, waterboy, cow-driver, stable groom, and perhaps printer's devil, not to mention assistant to Irwin Anderson, Sign Painter. Until the age of 11 he attended school regularly and was a rather good pupil, but from then on his attendance became erratic. Once he was excused for nine weeks, perhaps to help support the family after his father injured himself by falling into a ditch. In the school year of 1889-90, when Sherwood was 13 years old, he was late 32 times during the first term and 40 times during the second, undoubtedly because of his work as a newsboy. He became known as "Jobby" Anderson, the boy always on the run, and during his one year at high school he was often teased by the other pupils because of his many absences.

Though not so dreary as he would later paint it, the Anderson home could hardly satisfy a boy who was often invited to share the prosperity and cheerfulness of the Hurd family. Irwin Anderson could be fun for his children, but he was not the kind of father who would give them a sufficiently long period of security. Emma, trying to keep a half-dozen children fed, clothed, and respectable, had little time for, and not much training in, the social or cultural graces. But mutely and stubbornly she held the family together; her powerful if bruised will served as its centripetal core to an extent that sapped the energies she needed for herself. She was an intensely ambitious mother, and even if her ambitions were doomed to remain inarticulate, she saw to it that her children were brought up properly. Stella, a pretty girl of angular character, recited verses at the Presbyterian Church and in her late teens taught grade school at Clyde; Karl's gift for drawing was known throughout the town; and Sherwood was a popular figure, the responsible boy-merchant. Here, for Clyde, was visible proof that the children of even a former servant girl and a ne'er-do-well could rise if only they worked hard enough.

In the Anderson home there were few books (*The Pilgrim's Progress*, Tennyson's poems) but Sherwood, a furious if not well-directed reader, borrowed books from the Clyde school superintendent. Both Herman Hurd and Irving Anderson were to remember Sherwood as a constant reader during boyhood, a fact which lends credence to Sherwood's own recollection that "I went fishing with a book under my arm, went to ball games and read in a book between innings. There being few books in our house, I went book borrowing throughout the town." But this book-hunger should not be taken as a sign of precocious intellectuality; it indicated rather that a boy thrust too quickly and perilously into the world was eager to find a means of both extending and pleasantly escaping his narrow experience. He read whatever he could find, but no one taught him how or what to read—the painful struggle for that knowledge was to come much later. What little culture Clyde had was largely a veneer for its aspirations to moral propriety or worldly status, and Sherwood was too vital a boy not to sense the falsity of that veneer. Any healthy human being would have chosen Clyde's practice of commerce to its pretensions to culture.

Sherwood Anderson spent much of his mature life trying to relate himself to his boyhood in Clyde, which awed him almost as if it were a folk legend; at least five of his books are directly concerned with his youth and most of the others are crowded with its echoes. This self-absorption was partly due to his vanity; partly to a plausible belief that his life so impinged on a crucial era of American experience that it might be taken as representative of that era; and partly to a shrewd insight that the story of his career, as a classical instance of the untutored American's struggle to become an artist, could be absorbed into the democratic myth and thereby insure him an immortality his writings might not.

From Anderson's autobiographical volumes it is possible to extract almost everything but reliable information. As he himself blithely warned his readers, he made no effort to be accurate: he was recording the legend of his life rather than its mere events. That he justified this procedure by a dubious theory of art is, for the moment, irrelevant. What is important is that he felt some deep need to construct an elaborate public legend about his family and his boyhood self.

When Anderson could shape his memories into a tolerable pattern, when he could align them with the conception he had created of his self, the legend was not too far from the actuality and the distance between the two could be ascribed to a fairly innocent pleasure in romantic invention. Nor was such an occasional acceptance of his past due merely to sentimental self-gratification; he was able to write objectively about many of the aspects of his youth and later life that must have been distasteful to him. But when he touched those memories of boyhood which he could not order, those remembrances of his parents which invoked the most fundamental conflicts of his psychic history, he fell not merely into contradictions to fact but also into gaping inconsistencies within the legend itself. At precisely those points where it jarred the most intimate and sensitive nerves of memory, the legend was least under control.

Anderson was not, in any usual sense of the word, a liar. He was under no obligation to make life easy for future biographers, and he had, as he claimed for himself, the right to "arrange" his own past quite as he arranged the past of one of his fictional characters. But if his autobiographies cannot be read as records they can be taken as evidence, and if they often deviate from factual accuracy they as often penetrate to psychological truth. Anderson's portraits of his life in Clyde, of his mother and father, were retributive and nostalgic, qualities hardly conducive to accuracy; but there is in them, nonetheless, a somewhat buried group of insights which is partly a conscious issue of his mind and partly derived from the subterranean workings of his memory.

The usual stresses of family relationships impressed themselves on the boy Sherwood all the more deeply in that those relationships were disordered or, at the least, unconventional. His brothers and sisters impinged on him very strongly, though in ways that would not become thoroughly clear until adulthood, when each of them would come to represent, as if by some ironic prearrange-

ment, a significant side of his personality. As yet, however, he felt them mainly in their bulk: in the Anderson
house brothers and sister meant crowded rooms and a
struggle for space, competitors for food, clothing, and affection, unavoidable witnesses of all one did, and, in
times of trouble, comrades linked by a need to sustain
a shaken sense of family pride. In his recollections Anderson was to describe the atmosphere of his home as
loveless, but loveless it was not at all; rather was it aspir-
ing and strained in its aspirations, protective and harsh
in its protectiveness.

Karl Anderson, who has survived all of his younger
brothers, has said that Sherwood's portrait of his mother
was more faithful to the reality than that of his father.
Karl was right, for to Sherwood, both as boy and then
as man weighing boyhood, his mother was less perplexing
and more acceptable than his father.

The distortions to which the mature Anderson subjected the memory of his mother were all of one kind
and all the result of one feeling: he strengthened her
character while softening her features, he made her more
worthy of his love not because he doubted her worth but
because one tribute of guilt is idealization. He had not
loved her enough as a boy, he had taken her long silences
as tokens of distance, he had failed to see her suffering
and endurance—and now he would recompense her even
if she could no longer receive his gifts. In his books Anderson described the courage and fatalism with which his
mother had pulled the body of a drowned child from a
water barrel; years later a careful scholar discovered that
in actuality she had been overcome and ineffective. Anderson gleefully told how his mother would tease boys into

throwing cabbages at her door on Hallowe'en nights and would then store the cabbages for the coming winter; years later the same meticulous scholar reported that Sherwood had probably fabricated the story, an opinion shared by Karl Anderson. When a student wrote Anderson in 1939, asking which experience in his life he remembered with the greatest pleasure, he replied: "I think it is the memory of my mother coming to my bedside at night." In *A Story Teller's Story* he recalled how his mother would come at night to rub her children's hands with "warm, comforting melted fat. . . . The strange, silent woman! . . . The rubbing of the fat into the cracked hands of her son is a caress." Here he had dipped into the unconscious resources of the race, for the archetypal caress is a collective datum as well as an individual memory, the same in Combray as in Clyde.

Emma Anderson was hardly as silent as Sherwood said, and certainly not so strange. Her neighbors remembered her as a friendly woman, and as for the strangeness—was it really so strange in 19th-century America for a small-town wife to bear her burdens patiently, was it so strange that she continued to offer affection to the husband who often failed her? Emma gave whatever she could to her children, and to Sherwood she seemed—this "rather silent woman" whose health was being destroyed by heavy work, childbearing, and worry—the one certainty in a very uncertain life. More than the usual filial tie was to bind him to his memory of her. As he later recalled his boyhood she seemed its one true and indestructible pillar; she became the woman-image of his life and in that sense he remained forever faithful to her.

But his memories of his father could not be so simple or consistent. When the adult Anderson thought of his father, he was beset by a confusion of feelings: resentment, pleasure, and fear.. All his life Sherwood mused about his father, trying again and again to face the apparently uncomplicated fact that he was Irwin Anderson's son.

For a proud and strong-willed boy, such as Sherwood was in the late 1880's, nothing could have been more painful than to observe the blend of amused tolerance and mild condescension with which Clyde treated his father. Irwin Anderson was considered a "good sport," convivial, imaginative, and indulgent; he was always at hand for a G.A.R. celebration or a Fourth of July ceremony; but he was hardly the sort of man who could gain the thorough approval of a town dedicated to progress and industry. He was "too irresponsible"—and neither Sherwood nor Clyde cared to determine where that irresponsibility was an actual lapse of family obligation and where mere playfulness.

In many ways Sherwood could not avoid liking his father. Irwin responded quickly to adolescent feeling; by comparison with most townspeople and farmers he had a certain dash and style—even if his dash and style were sometimes employed to glide over failures as the head of a family; and he charmed and amused even when he most irritated and shamed one. If only this father could also have had dignity, if only Sherwood could have felt as proud of him publicly as he was fond of him privately. Sherwood could never quite understand how his father managed to "get by" and why his mother so seldom complained about him. In a curious way Emma was responsible for some of Sherwood's confusion of attitude:

the example of her bearing aroused in him critical perceptions of his father which she herself seldom cared to
express.

In his old age Herman Hurd was to recall an incident which reveals a great deal about Sherwood's boyhood situation. The older Anderson boys were working
with their father on a painting job, but instead of doing
his share of the work Irwin told his sons stories about the
Civil War. Exasperated, Sherwood threw his brush to the
ground and swore never again to paint for him. Is it too
improbable a guess to suppose that as the boy fumed at
Irwin's laziness he also enjoyed the memory of his stories? That was the source of his perplexity and irritation:
he could not even experience the pleasure of disliking
his father so thoroughly as he often felt he should.

In later years Sherwood recalled that his father "was
a man who was never alone. Before he went broke, running a harness shop, there were always a lot of men loaf-
ing in the shop. He went broke, of course, because he
gave too much credit. He couldn't refuse it and I
thought he was a fool. I had got to hating him." That
Irwin lost his shop through giving too much credit or
that the boy Sherwood, who could not then have been
more than 8 years old, was in a position to evaluate his
father's business policies is greatly open to doubt. But
if the first and the last sentences of the above passage
are read together they tell more about Sherwood's feelings toward his father than he could possibly have
guessed. To as critical-minded and relatively worldly a
boy as Sherwood, Irwin's loud boasting in the presence
of other men could only have been distasteful. Sherwood
might like him for his boyish camaraderie at home, but

he wanted a father who lived up to the public image of what a father should be.

About Irwin Anderson a great many legends have survived, most of them in Sherwood's books. His father, Sherwood wrote, had once become a book salesman specializing in General Grant's *Memoirs*. Herman Hurd remembered that Irwin, while preparing to act in an amateur theatrical, had become so drunk on stage-light alcohol that he could not perform his role. And Sherwood remembered that his father had toured the countryside one year with a magic-lantern show and a song-and-dance act, parasitically living off indulgent farmers while the family in Clyde was near destitution. Where does truth end and fancy begin? That Irwin peddled Grant's *Memoirs* is unlikely though not impossible (perhaps Sherwood was bemused by the vision of his father selling a book Mark Twain had published). The alcohol story is almost certainly untrue, a legend built around Irwin's tippling. But the recollection of Irwin as a touring vaudevillian apparently has some basis in fact, since Sherwood's younger brother, Ray, who violently objected to Sherwood's more fanciful reminiscences, also remembered the magic-lantern show. Irwin was the sort of man to be drawn to theatrical performances; as late as 1898 he acted in a Clyde production of *Old Glory in Cuba*, a fervidly patriotic drama. But it hardly matters whether one or another of these stories is true, for the mere fact that they could be remembered by Clyde residents and recorded by Sherwood is proof enough that Irwin Anderson was no ordinary small-town citizen.

Just as the boy's feelings for the father were confused, so the adult's recollections of those feelings were inconsistent. Anderson's first book *Windy McPherson's Son*, which appeared in 1916, began with a vindictive portrait of his father full of direct resentment and aggression. During the early 1920's when he was relatively secure in his fame and therefore inclined to an indulgent attitude toward the past, Anderson romanticized his father. In *A Story Teller's Story* the "windy" father became a man "who always wanted lovely things for people" and in whose "utter disregard for the facts of life" there was "something magnificent." Anderson could now gladly, forgivingly refer to "all such fellows as father and myself," for Irwin had become a symbol of justification for his own career and life, also not without their elements of irresponsibility. In the *Memoirs* Anderson was more restrained, trying to achieve a balanced memory of boyhood: it was "only after I had become a mature man, long after our mother's death, that I began to appreciate our father and to understand somewhat his eternal boyishness, his lack of the feeling of responsibility to others, his passion for always playing with life. . . ." But it is a question whether Anderson actually did find that balance or was merely suppressing the ambivalent feelings he had carried since childhood. As late as 1938 he wrote:

> I am sure that my bitterest disappointment was with my father. I went once into the country with him and we stayed over night at a camp where there were several men and women gathered. This was on the shore of Lake Erie . . . and there, during the night, I discovered that my father was having an affair with one of the women and was being untrue to my mother.

If such memories were accurate, then Anderson's admission that "I had got to hating him" is easily under-

standable; if they were invented, then beneath his retro-
spective vilification there must have been an even more
aggrieved resentment of his father than he ever dared express. But it seems most unlikely that a grown man could
have so persistently fastened his mind on alternately sentimental and aggressive memories unless there was a strong
warrant for them in his experience. Anderson dramatized,
romanticized, and exaggerated, but his memories of his
father were rooted in an original boyhood ambivalence. As
he admitted in later years, "often I was filled with bitterness,
and sometimes I wished he wasn't my father. I'd even in-
vent another man as my father." Such memories might
be embroidered, they could hardly be invented.

The boy Sherwood loved his mother without qualifica-
tion in a way he could never love his father, yet he identified himself with his father in a way he never could
with his mother. In later years that identification had its
pleasant aspects: it was charming to think that one's
father had also been a story-teller, a wanderer, a man
accused of irresponsibility by those who failed to understand him. But it was also frightening, for always there
was to lurk in Sherwood's mind the painful thought that
he had in him something of Irwin Anderson the idler
and boaster—the very Irwin Anderson he had so often rejected as a boy. In boyhood Sherwood could not find in
his father the total security he should have found; in
manhood he could not take the final step to loving the
memory of his father completely.

Emma Anderson, burned out by work and tuberculosis,
died in May 1895 at the age of 43. The Anderson home,
which had already begun to come apart when Karl left

Clyde, now disintegrated rapidly, and Sherwood could rightly feel that his boyhood had come to an end. In *Tar*, his fictional reminiscence, there is a description of this period which may be accepted as roughly accurate:

> The Moorehead house, with Tar's mother nowadays always half ill and growing constantly weaker, was no place for such a one as Dick [the father]. Now the woman of the house was living on her nerve. She was living because she did not want to die, not yet. Such a woman grows very determined and silent. The husband, more than his children, feels her silence as a kind of reproach. God, what can a man do?

For several years Sherwood had been doing odd jobs in Clyde, but as long as Emma stubbornly maintained a home he did not face the need to assume the role of independent manhood. Now there was no alternative. Before her death Emma had exacted a promise from her only daughter, Stella, that she would keep the family together. Stella tried but the task was beyond her capacities; she resented the burden suddenly thrust on her, and her emotional acerbity, apparently her dominant character trait, prevented her from serving as a center for the family. For about a year Sherwood remained in Clyde, working, he later claimed, as a stable groom, and then he took the step which most ambitious midwestern boys of his day sooner or later had to take: he left home for the big city.

Sherwood spent about a year and a half in Chicago, from late 1896 to the spring of 1898. It was not a happy time. His job rolling barrels of apples in a cold-storage warehouse tired him excessively, and since his pay was low he had to share a tenement apartment with Cliff and Jeanette Paden, son and daughter of a former Clyde mayor. (Cliff Paden was later to be known as John Emerson, an affluent movie producer whose career came to represent for Anderson a tempting but rejected choice.) Jeanette Paden was later to recall that "he talked about his unhappiness all the time." *The Clyde Enterprise* announced, however, that "Jobby" Anderson had "a lucrative position in Chicago"—perhaps because that was what "Jobby" was telling the folks back home.

When it seemed that the United States might actively fight Spain, Sherwood, who had joined the National Guard in 1895, wrote his militia captain: "If by any chance this war scare amounts to anything, and the company is called, please telegraph me . . . and I will be with you." But when the war came he enlisted "because I was broke and could see no other way to avoid going back into a factory." To his brother Karl he wrote at the time, "I prefer yellow fever in Cuba to living in cold storage in Chicago." When he returned to Clyde he was received "as a local hero . . . rushing to my country's defense. I am afraid it was bunk."

Clyde spared no pains in behalf of its soldiers. "The ladies of Clyde," reported the *Enterprise*, "prepared a magnificent banquet. . . . Addresses were made by the local clergy and attorneys. . . . The scene was one long to be remembered and several ladies were overcome and had to be carried from the hall." Sherwood enjoyed what he could, and among his pleasures was a brief affair with a Clyde girl before he moved off with Company I of the Sixth Ohio Infantry. In May 1898 the Company was accepted into federal service and from then until the end of the year it trained in southern army camps. In early

January 1899 it landed at Cienfuegos, Cuba, and remained there for four dreary months of patrol duty.
Sherwood was popular among his army comrades, who
remembered him as a fellow given to prolonged reading,
mostly in dime westerns and historical romances, and tal-
ented at finding a girl when he wanted one. For the first
of these traits he was frequently teased, but the second
brought him the respect it usually does in armies.

By May Anderson was back in Clyde. The townspeople, including his father, gave its untested heroes a lively
welcome, and the fierce *Enterprise* consoled its readers
with the remark that "it is not their fault that they were
not in battle." But there was now little reason for him
to remain in Clyde. His brothers were scattered through
the Midwest: Irving had taken Sherwood's old job as
barrel-roller in Chicago, Karl had found employment
as cover illustrator for *The Woman's Home Companion*
in Springfield, Ohio, where the magazine then had its
office, and only Ray, the least industrious of the brothers,
was still in Clyde. A few days after his return Sherwood
went to Springfield to discuss his future with Karl who
by then, as in later years, was the actual head of the
family. Sherwood, according to Karl's recollection, "was
very thin, all skin and bones, and I could see that something was troubling him. Finally he confessed that he
was in doubt about his future, and that he felt he should
have a better education." Karl suggested that he go the
following fall to Wittenberg Academy, a preparatory
school in Springfield. During the summer Sherwood worked
on a farm near Clyde and in the fall he left for Wittenberg.
Except for one or two brief visits, he was never to return
to the town of his boyhood.

Sherwood Anderson was now 23 years old, a handsome young man of swarthy complexion whose most striking feature was a pair of sunken, luminous black eyes. Though lively in temperament and spontaneously friendly, he seemed without any visible prospects in the world: he was poorly educated, his ambition was diffused, he had no trade. A thoroughly unremarkable young man and a rather backward one if judged by the standards he then accepted, Anderson knew that if he was to make anything of his life he would have to do it quickly. Behind him was Clyde, the town which had provided the setting for his most important experience, and the dead mother and discarded father who were forever to be the most important figures in his life. The vise of memory would hold him tightly and insistently, and, as he later wrote of George Willard's departure from Winesburg, his boyhood life in Clyde would forever remain "a background on which to paint the dreams of manhood."

Success and Consequences

SOON after entering the Wittenberg Academy, Anderson had to face a problem which, in varying ways, would remain with him throughout his life. At the age of 23 he could hardly have been assigned to any but the senior class, but because it was almost a decade since his year in high school he was less familiar with the academic subject-matter than the other, younger students. Since his prestige obviously depended on his success as a student and since in any case he had decided to improve his mind, he studied diligently. In his five subjects (English, Latin, German, Geometry, and Physics) he was a preponderantly "A" student. What later became of the knowledge acquired at Wittenberg is something of a mystery, for in his mature life Anderson could not read a foreign language, had difficulty in coping with English spelling and grammar, and extended his ignorance of science into a virtual creed.

Once he realized he could compete with the other students, Anderson thoroughly enjoyed his year at Wittenberg. Together with Karl he lived in a boardinghouse, "The Oaks," which served as a center for young artists, writers, and teachers. Here for the first time he met people who talked stimulatingly about books, who hoped to leave commercial jobs and devote themselves to creative work, and who gave him a glimpse, although a very restricted one, of a new and attractive world of culture. Two of the boarders, Marco Morrow, a magazine editor, and George Daugherty, a newspaperman, became Anderson's lifelong friends. At "The Oaks" Sherwood earned part of his tuition by working as a house-boy and, according to Daugherty, quickly became a favorite of the boarders "as he went about the leisurely performance of his duties, tending the stoves, filling the kerosene lamps, going out on errands. He was respectful to his elders, even to Morrow and me, who were only a few years his senior. He had wit, original viewpoints, no bumptiousness—and a certain magnetism." That Anderson could then have expressed "original viewpoints" is doubtful, but the remainder of Daugherty's description is quite credible.

In the spring of 1900 Anderson was one of eight class orators at the Wittenberg commencement ceremonies. He spoke on "Zionism," a subject about which his ignorance could have been no greater than that of his audience. "I got it all out of books," he was to recall, "I spent days in the library, cramming for it. . . . I walked up and down in a room, practising, making gestures." The oration, said the *Springfield Republic-Times*, was "a plea for the Jew . . . finely worded, scholarly." Still more impressed was Harry Simmons, advertising manager for *The Woman's Home Companion*, who, after hearing Anderson, impulsively offered him a job in the magazine's

Chicago office. Anderson accepted, of course, and, convinced that he was at last to be the rising young businessman, quickly left for Chicago. But, since his immediate superior disliked him, the job proved a disappointment, and soon Sherwood was looking for a new place. He found one when Marco Morrow, who had recently come to Chicago to work for the Frank White advertising agency, persuaded his employers to hire Anderson as a copywriter. In 1903 the White company was absorbed into the Long-Critchfield agency, and there Anderson worked the next three years.

As a copywriter Anderson was an immediate success. The advertising business was then abandoning its dignified 19th-century approach and assuming that intimate wheedling tone which would soon become a staple of American salesmanship. To this new trend Anderson, who was especially gifted at composing sly mail-order lures, quickly adapted himself. In Chicago advertising circles he was considered a promising young man "whose achievements often bordered on the spectacular in handling such accounts as the Long-Critchfield organization placed under his direction . . . he was forever bringing some ailing business back to normal by ingenious exploitation of [his] lively imagination." The author of these lines, a Chicago copywriter recalling his profession's days of early glory, recalled with glee how Anderson had saved a faltering buggy firm from bankruptcy by promising each mail-order customer a buggy originally made for the firm's president.

And so, of a sudden [Anderson has written] I am lifted up into a new world of well-dressed young men.

As it turns out I couldn't sell advertising but I could write advertisements.

. . . I buy new clothes, hats, shoes, socks, shirts. I walk freely on Michigan Boulevard in Chicago, go to drinking parties, meet bigger and bigger business men.

I create nothing. I boost, boost. . . .

I strut, carry a cane. I let my hair grow long, aim to be a bit original in my dress. . . . I begin to wear spats. I even buy a dinner coat.

The pleasures of good food and distinguished clothes, the opportunities to mingle with men "on top," the hope that at last he was absorbing something of the worldliness for which he had yearned—these experiences made Anderson's life seem sweet. Raises in pay came fairly often, and in the Chicago advertising world Anderson's blend of shrewd braggadocio and naïve optimism made him popular.

He grew vain, boasting that he could "sell anything" by mail and promising the office girls at Long-Critchfield that he would find husbands for them through his enticing letters. In those years "there was a good deal of talk of the nobility of business. . . . The word *service* had begun to be used. I went in enthusiastically. There was a side of my nature, a certain great plausibility, a trick of winning men's confidence that made me rather succeed from the first." It seemed as if "Jobby" had found his job.

During 1903 and 1904 Anderson contributed more than a dozen articles to *Agricultural Advertising*, a trade journal published by Long-Critchfield. He wrote two signed columns, "Rot and Reason," a series of Rotarian puffs, and "Business Types," semifictional personality sketches.

These articles show full-face the Anderson who appointed
himself a champion of the American businessman, the
very Anderson against whom he was to spend the bulk of
his later life in rebellion. One of his first pieces was
headed, "Push, Push, Push," and a particularly interesting one is a polemic against Henry George, that "dismal
prophet," in which he gave a classically ingenuous exposi-
tion of the businessman's outlook:

> There is the labor question and the Negro question
> and the ever present money question . . . and mean-
> while the businessmen of the world go quietly ahead
> . . . doing the work of the week and the day, while
> the reformers and preachers and politicians talk and
> mix new cure-alls for the ailing body politic. One
> good, clean-minded businessman, who gets down to
> work cheerfully in the morning, who treats the people
> about him with kindness and consideration, who wor-
> ries not about world-politics, who faces the small ills
> of his day . . . is probably doing more downright
> good than all of the canting moralists who ever
> breathed. . . .

Somewhat more realistic was another piece in which Anderson admitted:

> Now, in the advertising business, when we speak of
> success, the word can mean but one thing. There is
> only one kind of business success, and that is, the kind
> of success that makes money.

Sometimes he could reach lyrical heights:

> As a man travels about he realizes more and more
> that the businessman is the very front and center of
> things American. He is the man on horseback in our
> national life. He knows, and I pray you, doubt not,
> that he dictates the whole works. . . . And what man-

ner of man is he, this American businessman? Is he a
better, cleaner and braver man than the warriors and
scholars who have cast their big shadows in the past?
You can be sure he is.

Perhaps encouraged by the favorable response to his
articles in *Agricultural Advertising*, Anderson branched
out with two contributions to *The Reader*, a popular
monthly magazine. Entitled "A Business Man's Reading"
and "The Man and His Books," these articles urged businessmen to read widely in order to advance their careers.
The sketches Anderson wrote in 1904 for *Agricultural
Advertising*, while they are stylistically as dismal as those
of the previous year, suggest at least the slightly more ambitious aim of portraying human types met in the business
world. Thus "The Good Fellow" is

> probably a fat man and it is sure he sleeps at night. . . .
> The real good fellow, like the real poet, is born, not
> made. His the pleasant, ringing laugh, his the cheerful
> belief in other men's honesty and good intent. . . .
> Off with your hats then to this genial soul, he of the
> smile and the words of cheer, and may the advertising
> game yearly find in its ranks more of this good breed
> who are called good fellows, and are in reality only
> true born gentlemen after all.

Particularly in the earlier pieces he wrote for the Long-
Critchfield magazine Anderson accepted uncritically the
cant of the business world, sarcasm or irony about its values being then quite beyond his range of perception.
Both his own memories ("I boost, I boost") and the quite
sincere naïveté of the articles themselves indicate that
he believed what he wrote. Exactly when he began to
question himself and his work it is difficult to say, for in

the life of an insufficiently educated man such changes occur slowly and imperceptibly. Very probably he originally thought his "Business Types" worth writing and only gradually realized their shoddiness. Marco Morrow, who knew Anderson intimately in these years, has testified that before leaving the advertising agency in 1906 Anderson had begun to write fiction in free moments at work, on trips to agency customers and during week ends in country hotels. Once Anderson blithely informed Morrow that he would decide within two weeks whether to become a millionaire or an artist. "If only a man will put the making of money above all other things in life," said Anderson, he can soon become rich. And while an artistic career was not quite so easily achieved, he thought he might try writing or painting or sculpture. Knowing very little about any of these, he had no hesitation about plunging into all of them.

In early 1905 his articles were brought to the notice of Cyrus Curtis, publisher of *The Saturday Evening Post*, who thought them sufficiently promising to invite Anderson to contribute a manuscript. Anderson sent one but, according to Morrow, it was rejected because it failed to "glorify" the businessman. Apparently Anderson had by then partly discarded the views which had made him seem "promising" to Curtis. Yet in the May 1905 issue of *Agricultural Advertising* there is a report that at a Long-Critchfield banquet Sherwood Anderson spoke on how its employees could "make good" for the firm. Perhaps his tongue was by now deeply tucked into his cheek, but it is more likely that he was trapped in a genuine conflict of attitudes: he no longer wished to glorify the businessman, that "very front and center of things

American," and yet he still hoped to "make good." This contradiction, not exactly unknown in American life, was to gnaw at his life for at least the next seven years; he would hope to become a millionaire and an artist too.

The creative urge had begun to agitate Anderson's mind, and for 35 years it was never, not even in his most fallow periods, quite to desert him. Few Americans have ever dedicated themselves to the role of the artist with such deliberate solemnity, and that this role should have been chosen by an American at the very opposite pole of vocation must be cause for wonder and admiration. Sherwood Anderson was to be a writer—perhaps, as he later said, in response to a family gift and a family need for telling stories, perhaps as a result of having been exposed to the cosmopolitan atmosphere of Chicago, perhaps as a competitive reaction to his brother's painting, but most likely because the abuse of language inevitable to advertising often arouses in sensitive copywriters a desire to use it honestly and creatively.

Yet to put the matter so explicitly is surely to anticipate. In these years Anderson's main ambition was to improve his status in the outer world rather than to nourish his potentially creative self. In 1904 he had married Cornelia Lane, a well-educated young woman of prosperous family, who seemed to Anderson a personification of the qualities he lacked but was learning to admire—social refinement, cultural ease, personal assurance. And to her (here we can only speculate) Anderson may have been impressive because of his liveliness, his ambition, and his increasing interest in cultural matters.

At its outset the marriage was a happy one. Cornelia

provided Anderson with an attractive home, was a gracious hostess adept at the social niceties he was apt to overlook, and yet was no mere mindless housewife. Many of the social evenings at the Anderson home would turn into literary readings by the light of a fire. To a man in whose memory Clyde must still have been immediate, this atmosphere of genteel, but not at all philistine, culture was extremely pleasant and sustaining.

Inescapably, as his personality was planed by his wife's fine influence, Anderson became dissatisfied with his copywriting in which everything had to be garish and gross. "I decided," he has recalled, "to get out of advertising writing. There were too many lies being told. . . . I was afraid I would begin to believe the lies I wrote." Perhaps it would be more accurate to say that he was now beginning to disbelieve the lies he had written.

In the fall of 1906 he left his job at Long-Critchfield to become president of the United Factories Company in Cleveland, Ohio, a firm for which he had previously composed advertisements. Though his new post represented a rise in status, it was not so imposing as its title might suggest, for he was actually little more than a sales manager. The United Factories Company was a mail-order outlet for several factories producing such varied items as incubators, stoves, paints, and buggy tops. To increase the volume of its business Anderson wrote clever advertisements, particularly a catalogue in which he claimed that his company saved its customers money by dispensing with middlemen—an anticipation of a major theme in 20th century advertising.

In Cleveland Anderson was under constant and severe strain. He worked long hours trying to make up for his ignorance of office routine, and his "nervousness" was aggravated by the suppressed but still irksome split in his values. At home Cornelia continued the pattern of life she had begun in Chicago: literary evenings and on Sunday mornings French lessons. But suddenly Anderson's business suffered a serious failure: the incubators didn't incubate, angry farmers returned them by the hundreds, and though hardly responsible for the designing error in the incubators Anderson soon had to look for a new job. Meanwhile his wife gave birth to a son, Robert, and the weight of family responsibility began visibly to increase.

In the fall of 1907 Anderson, with wife and child, moved to Elyria, a drab town about 40 miles west of Cleveland, where he began his major experience as a businessman.

In Elyria Anderson persuaded merchants, bankers, and professional men to invest money in the Anderson Manufacturing Company, a mail-order firm selling a roof-paint called "Roof Fix." His company was capitalized at $200,000 but never had more than a small fraction of that sum at its disposal. To acquire more capital and to entice paint merchants into a binding relationship with his firm, Anderson worked out a scheme called "Commercial Democracy," according to which dealers in "Roof Fix" would purchase shares of his stock and thereby have a stake in the company's prosperity.

In his *Memoirs* Anderson has characteristically embroidered this scheme by describing it as the issue of vaguely socialist sentiments: "I began to publish a magazine called *Commercial Democracy*, writing the entire magazine myself; I spent money circulating it by thousands of copies. I went from town to town, preaching my idea of altruism in manufacturing . . . to retail merchants." Actually, *Commercial Democracy* was less a magazine than an adorned advertisement, and closer to the truth than the *Memoirs* is Anderson's admission about his stock-sharing plan that "I don't mean to say my ideas were clean. I kept thinking up little cheating schemes and putting them in operation at the same time I was preaching to myself and others against such schemes. . . ." Similarly, it would be easier to credit Anderson's claim that during his five-year stay in Elyria he wrote and destroyed a book called *Why I Am a Socialist* if his fiction written in the same period were not explicitly antisocialist.

But while *Commercial Democracy* did not flourish, Anderson's business did, and in 1908 and 1909 he seemed on the way to becoming a substantial entrepreneur. The rate of profit on "Roof Fix" was large, since it sold for five times its cost of production. Anderson wrote his own chatty advertising, distressingly similar to some of the less inspired literary productions of his last years. He worked hard, and in 1908 his company absorbed the paint manufacturer who had supplied it with paint. Under the circumstances, the fact that his barn paint peeled quickly could hardly have seemed important.

The Andersons soon slid into the conventions of small-town middle-class life. Cornelia joined a ladies' literary society, read papers at its meetings, and was admired as dignified, pleasant, and, above all, cultured. Both Sherwood and Cornelia attended meetings of the Round Table Club, a discussion group for young married people.

Sherwood became a regular golfer at the Elyria Country Club and a frequent pool player at the Elks' lodge. And on the last day of 1908 the Andersons welcomed another son, John. It seemed as if Sherwood had at last found his place in the world, as if all his affairs were thriving and all his responses conspicuously normal.

But the appearance was deceptive. For his first few years in Elyria Anderson was seriously committed to his dream of wealth, and there is no extravagance in his recollection that "I was going to be a rich man, establish my family. We were in this respectable house now, the biggest and best . . . I had ever lived in. . . . Next year a bigger house; and after that presently, a country estate." Yet Anderson could not long accept the role he had established for himself. The novelty of running a business quickly waned, the old vague stirrings to "express" himself could not be indefinitely suppressed, and most disturbing of all he felt that "I was telling people the same kind of lies I had lied before." Half-surreptitiously and soon quite openly he began to undermine his own status as a respectable businessman, destroying at night the image created by day. More and more frequently, he would retire to the attic each evening and write.

Of all the periods in Anderson's life, the one in Elyria was the most difficult for him to assess in his memory. He always felt a strong need to suggest that he had then enjoyed a considerably more critical view of himself than in fact he did, for these years in Elyria later seemed to him the most shameful of his life, the years when he acquiesced in the detestable values of the business world. Sometimes, however, he would deliberately darken his recollected Elyria personality, as if to say: see from what depths I have come, see how remarkable a revolution I have wrought in my life! Once he did strike very close to the truth about his Elyria experience when he wrote in his *Memoirs:* "I am representing myself here as a young American businessman, as a good deal of a Babbitt, but I was never completely that . . . the picture I am trying to give here is of a man not easy flowing, in fact terribly self-conscious." A good deal of a Babbitt but never completely one, and terribly self-conscious—that is accurate self-portraiture.

William Sutton, the academic biographer of Anderson's early years, has interviewed several residents of Elyria who remembered him from the 1907-12 period. The responses to Sutton's questions provide a vivid example of how mixed and confused were the impressions created by Anderson on both his business acquaintances and his friends. One of his secretaries thought him a man of intense ambition, shrewd and sharp in business affairs, and a rather hard employer who discharged inefficient workers without hesitation. Other employees remembered him as friendly and kindly. A personal friend recalled him as erratic in behavior, modernistic in taste, and perhaps a believer in "free love." Anderson's Elyria banker said that he "had a pleasing personality but lived in the clouds a good deal. . . . As I remember him, he was moody and self-contained, and we all considered him something of a nut."

These recollections may be partly distorted by a common assumption that for a paint manufacturer to become a "highbrow" writer he must originally have been "something of a nut." But unquestionably there is a particle of truth in each of them, and to put them side by side is merely to show that the Elyria Sherwood Anderson was a badly splintered personality. To his secretary he seemed fractious; to his friend daring, as by the standards of Elyria in 1908 he no doubt was; and to his banker impractical. Which is to say that he had no core of self controlling all of his relationships, but could only play a variety of conflicting and ultimately paralyzing roles.

To some extent Anderson was justified in feeling that his Elyria friends would neither understand nor sympathize with his dual existence as writer and businessman, but in his resentment of them there was also a projection of an inner uncertainty. For it is certainly not true, as he has written in *A Story Teller's Story*, that he "worked more or less in secret, as one might indulge in some forbidden vice." All of his friends knew about his writing and some even heard him read aloud portions of his first novel. In fact, the early drafts of *Windy McPherson's Son* and *Marching Men* were typed in his office by his secretary. The "forbidden vice" existed mainly in Anderson's mind.

To feel harried is, in effect, to be harried. Pressing psychological necessities may have led Anderson to exaggerate the antagonism his writing would arouse, but he was surely right in feeling that between his paint company and his fiction writing there was an irreconcilable conflict which could be relieved only by a decisive choice. To lessen the pressures of his anxiety and provide himself with intellectual companionship, he asked his youngest brother Earl, a sensitive and dreamy man, to come to Elyria. Since he was better educated than any of the Anderson brothers, Earl could talk of art and life in a way which Sherwood hungrily absorbed. Earl hoped to become a painter and it was from him, Sherwood later said, that he learned "the impulses and purposes of the artist." Together they would take long walks or buggy trips at night, talking of their ambitions and buoying each other's hopes.

It was inevitable that Anderson's disturbed condition should damage his marriage. In his *Memoirs* Anderson has said that Cornelia was unsympathetic to his writing and feared it would endanger the security of the family. Karl Anderson has also recalled that Sherwood told him "his wife gave scant approval to his attempts at writing." These versions clash head-on with the memory of a friend of the Andersons in Elyria, Florence Terry, who has recalled that "it is certainly untrue that she [Cornelia] ever discouraged Sherwood's writing efforts, but on the contrary, did all she could to help and encourage him . . . he knew his limitations in a cultural way and expressed great appreciation of his wife . . . for her help in diction, rhetoric, etc. [Cornelia] never tried to interfere with his individual liberty and never criticized Sherwood. . . ."

In the *Memoirs* Anderson has unwittingly provided a clue to the probable truth about his relations with his wife: "the woman I had married was educated. She had traveled in Europe while I . . . to tell the truth I could at that time just spell the simplest words—I was a man just out of the laboring class and to the American middleclass that was then, and is perhaps yet, a disgrace." That Anderson's spelling could have been any worse than in his later years seems incredible, but the point of this passage is that it reveals a man whose poor education had caused him to feel the burden of inferiority. As Anderson showed his wife his first manuscripts, she was naturally quick to notice their obvious mechanical errors, and to him that must have been a bitter, if suppressed, humiliation. Despite the fact that he retrospectively damned her attitude as snobbish ("middleclass"), he may well have suspected that there *was* something presumptuous in his daring to write. For he did make gross errors and Cornelia did have to correct them.

When a third child, Marion, was born in 1911, Cornelia must have worried still more about the effect of her husband's writing on his capacity as breadwinner—as she had reason to worry. No doubt, she was also skeptical of his talent as a writer. And since Anderson himself shared both her worry and her skepticism, what simpler recourse could he have than in all sincerity to believe that she was antagonistic to his painfully wrought work? From there it was only a step to the feeling that she was an impediment to his becoming an accomplished writer.

But the real problem was Anderson's alone and had little to do with Cornelia's attitude toward his work. To put it most simply, his problem was to make up his mind. One way or another, for good or bad, he needed a set of sustaining and guiding values; without them he would spend increasing amounts of time at bars or on "business trips" to Cleveland. And as he hesitated, "the illness inside me grew."

On November 27, 1912 Anderson told his secretary, "My feet are cold and wet. I have been walking too long on the bed of a river." A few minutes later he left the factory. He walked out of the town, and for four days he aimlessly wandered about until, on December 1, he was

found in Cleveland by a pharmacist. The following day
The Cleveland Leader wrote:

> Wandering gypsy-like about the countryside after
> disappearing from his home in Elyria four days ago,
> walking almost incessantly save for a few hours of
> sleep snatched in thickets and all the while uncon-
> scious of his identity, Sherwood Anderson . . . was
> discovered late yesterday afternoon in a drug store
> at E. 152 St. . . .
> Anderson was found by a physician to be suffering
> from the effects of some severe mental strain and was
> taken by friends to Huron Road Hospital. . . .
> Anderson is about thirty-seven years old, but looked
> older, with a several days' growth of beard on his face
> and haggard lines resulting from his unusual fatigue
> and exposure. . . .

A few days later *The Cleveland Leader* reported that

> Elyria friends . . . were of the belief yesterday that
> Anderson had broken down under the strain of work
> on a novel, which was to have been his masterpiece.
> . . . Physicians refuse to diagnose his case further than
> to say that he has suffered a nervous breakdown from
> overwork. . . .

Considerable insight into the nature of this breakdown
is provided by two pieces of writing, one apparently
mailed by Anderson to his wife during his wanderings
from Elyria to Cleveland and the other partly written
and partly dictated by him while in the Cleveland hospital. Though it is now not possible to quote or paraphrase
these documents, a few pervasive psychological motifs
may be observed in them: a violent aggression against his
role as an adult male and against the intimate relationships accompanying that role; an identification with

a famous literary hero traditionally associated with in-decision and melancholy; a regression to early levels of childhood feeling in a way which suggests a too sharp withdrawal of maternal attentions; and a generalized con-fusion as to sex role which is manifested in symbols in-dicating a retreat from masculinity and a cringing be-fore imagined feminine assaults.

Anderson recovered quickly from his breakdown, or at least from its more dramatic manifestations, for on De-cember 6 the *Elyria Evening Telegram*, under the head-ing "Sherwood Anderson Will Write Book on His Ex-perience as 'Nomad,'" printed an article including the following paragraph:

> He knew his identity but could not disclose it; he wanted to return home but could tell no person of his desires. . . . Mr. Anderson through deep thought threw himself into the trance. "It is dangerous but it will be a good story and the money will always be welcome," said he.

Even if one discounts the fantastic reference to self-hypnosis as a consequence of deep thought, this report in-dicates that a few days after his hospitalization Anderson had already begun his lifelong effort to veil from the public, and probably from himself, the true nature of his breakdown. He was to sponsor the legend that the breakdown had been partly genuine and partly feigned; some years later he told Margaret Anderson, editor of the *Little Review*, that it had been a case of "conscious aphasia," whatever odd affliction that may be. In Harry Hansen's vivid but inaccurate sketch of Anderson the breakdown is described as a "maneuver" arranged to-gether with a Cleveland doctor—no doubt because that was what Anderson wanted Hansen to believe and print. By the time Anderson wrote his *Memoirs* he portrayed the breakdown as a mere trick: "The thought occurred to me that if men thought me a little insane they would forgive me if I lit out. . . ." And in a recent reprint of *Winesburg* this version is naïvely repeated: "The main event in Anderson's life was when he suddenly walked out of his job as manager of a paint factory in Elyria, Ohio—deliberately leaving behind him the impression that he had lost his mind."

This is the great Anderson legend, deliberately cultivated and eagerly received, repeated in any number of popular and scholarly accounts of his life. It is a legend that has sunk deeply into the American imagination, for it is profoundly relevant to the emotional climate of American life, to the half-suppressed yearnings with which so many Americans wear out their lives. But, alas, it is only a legend. The truth, as Karl Anderson has written, is that there "was nothing deliberate" in Sherwood's breakdown. It was quickened by business worries, immediately provoked by an inability to choose a consistent course of life, and based on a fundamental psychic maladjustment in his private life. The legend, on the other hand, was a dramatization of a later decision to devote himself to art—and it is not difficult to understand why Anderson should have preferred the world to believe that at the age of 36 he made a bold change in his style of life, similar to Gauguin's a quarter of a century before him. But perhaps by way of extenuation, if extenuation is ever relevant or necessary in such matters, one might recall that Anderson was beset by his dilemma, not in Paris, but in Elyria, Ohio.

"A Will to Splendor"

WHATEVER its genesis or economy, Anderson's breakdown had at least one beneficial outcome: he could no longer continue the double life of business by day and writing by night which had fractured his emotional life. With his business near collapse and his reputation in Elyria heavily stained, he had no choice but to leave for Chicago and there to look for work as a copy-writer. Shortly after being hired by his old employers, now reorganized as the Taylor-Critchfield agency, he brought his wife and children to Chicago.

On the face of it, Anderson was merely descending in status from businessman to employee, but actually the change was motivated by a deep and liberating clarification of values. In an unpublished autobiographical fragment, Anderson had recalled that he told Bayard Barton, head of the agency: "You know I do not believe in advertising. . . . I think I can come back to the agency and keep my mouth shut. You know I am a good [copy] writer. I can fake. . . . Do you want to employ me?" Barton, who himself nursed literary ambitions, was both irritated and touched by Anderson's frankness, and subsequently permitted him a very considerable leeway in his work.

Copy-writing was now the only way Anderson could earn his living, but for the first time he could also say in full consciousness: "When I am being corrupt, perverting the speech of men, let me remain aware of what I am doing . . . hypocrisy in this matter, this believing your own bunk, [is] the real sin against the Holy Ghost." Circumstances forced him to write detested advertisements, but his conscious self was now largely directed toward the goal of art. He would repeatedly be tempted by success and his writing would always be uniquely concerned with the need to resist that temptation, but never would he deviate from the choice he had made.

During the next several years, from 1913 until almost the end of the decade, Anderson produced a considerable amount of new writing, revised his older work, and —what is so extraordinary for a man of much egotism and little training—discarded a good deal of it. From Elyria he brought four novels, *Windy McPerson's Son*, *Many Marriages*, *Mary Cochran*, and *Talbot Whittingham*, the latter two never to be published. To *Mary Cochran* he returned in 1919 but could extract from it only the story "Unlighted Lamps." *Talbot Whittingham* became almost an obsession, since there are extant at least half a dozen drafts, some of them reworked in the 1930's. When he was honest with himself Anderson had a shrewd critical sense of what was good and bad in his own work, and it is to his credit that in later years he refrained from foisting his early manuscripts on publishers.

In Chicago he wrote with a harried fury and apparently

unlimited energy. Now in his late thirties, he knew so much less than the young writers he was beginning to meet, he had read so much less than most of them, he had wasted so many years that his only recourse was to work deep into the nights, seizing every minute he could. To his friends he seemed jaunty and gay, but he was a man whose ambition exacerbated and in turn fed on anxiety about his future. "I gave as little as I could to my job, continually saving myself for writing, faking a good deal, being frank at least with my employers as to what I was doing." Fortunately, he could turn out copy quickly and then use the rest of his work day for his own writing. When sent to an out-of-town advertiser, Anderson would outrageously flatter the man's product and then cajole him into requesting Taylor-Critchfield to let him write copy "on the spot" for a week. Most of the week Anderson would then devote to his own work. To George Daugherty, also employed at the Taylor-Critchfield agency, Anderson once compared himself to a schoolboy who set a geography in front of him and drew caricatures of the teacher behind it. At the agency he shrewdly cultivated the notion that he was an eccentric genius ("the greatest unpublished novelist in America") who could not be expected to observe the same routine, or the same hours, as the other copy-writers. "I wore loud and flaming ties. I had got somewhere a huge ring and slipped my ties through this and wore it at my neck." When Anderson published his first story, an anemic affair called "The Rabbit Pen," in *Harper's*, his prestige among the advertising men rose still higher. He was their local genius, their apology for themselves.

Two aims now dominated Anderson's life: to "catch up" with his new literary friends, and to be "free" of social responsibilities, whether to employer, wife, or children. His taste formed by the better standards of the time, he began systematically to read such writers as Wells, Bennett, Hardy, and Moore. He listened eagerly to the conversations of the literary people, and, unable to compete with them on their own terms, began to evolve his characteristic literary personality: the rooted folk-poet. To become, at last, the Unbound Artist, to gain the freedom for which a whole generation was panting and straining, Anderson had to slash ties deeper than most of the young Chicago writers could possibly have known. He was no carefree young man who, without much pain or hardship, could marry and unmarry; he was in his late thirties, the father of three children.

Sometimes, when he thought of his situation, he suffered stabs of his old guilt: "Could it be that by acceptance of the fact of a rather unscrupulous and dishonorable quality in myself I had got a new freedom?" Could it be that even the act of leaving Elyria was an evasion of responsibility? In the winter of 1913 Anderson was again a perilously sick man, and to rest his nerves, write without interruption, and perhaps patch up a torn marriage, he took a long "vacation." Together with Cornelia he went to the Ozarks, where he lived in a shack and tried to regain some mental stability. In the spring of 1914 he returned to Chicago, sporting a beard and wearing his trousers tucked into big boots—nothing could so impress the city literati as the sight of a homespun American writer. He had not written much in the Ozarks, it had been too cold; but later he gravely told Harry Hansen and Hansen as gravely repeated in his *Midwest Portraits*, that he had completed a novel during the winter but had thrown it out of the win-

dow on the train to Chicago. At the advertising agency his
employers were becoming uneasy, for Anderson now
seemed rather too unconventional. They did not really
want him back, but by a ruse he managed to regain his job
—he *was* a good copy-writer.

His marriage dragged on for a few more months,
though both he and Cornelia must by now have realized
it was beyond repair. To him she represented, unavoid-
ably and almost impersonally, the life of paint factories,
ladies' literary clubs, and diapers. That this identification was
unfair hardly mattered: he needed a gesture to cap his
act of liberation, a gesture apparently emanating from his
conscious will rather than from a nervous breakdown, and
no gesture seemed so appropriate or so easily managed as
a separation from his wife. Cornelia tried hard to adapt herself to his new manner of life; she was patient, gracious,
ready to accept his new friends. When he contributed an
essay to the opening number of the *Little Review*, she also
wrote a book review for it. But the separation had to come,
and Cornelia accepted it with grace and courage. To support her three children she became a schoolteacher in a small
Indiana town—and Anderson knew yet another cause for
guilt. A few years later, when he was planning to widen his
range of magazine publication, he asked a New York literary person then visiting Chicago not to spread word of
his personal affairs in the East.

By mid-1914 Anderson was mixing freely with the
small literary groups that comprised the rising "Chicago
Renaissance." In the spring of 1913 his brother Karl had
taken him to a party at Floyd Dell's home, where he was
soon to be welcomed half as a curiosity and half as a
burgeoning genius by the young newspapermen, critics,

poets, and artists who gathered there. When Anderson read aloud from *Windy McPherson's Son*, Dell was rhapsodic: "A new, hitherto unknown novelist swam into my ken, with the manuscript of . . . *Windy McPherson's Son*, which I immensely admired; it had things in it about the Middle West which had never got into fiction, and a soul-searching quasi-Dostoievskian note in it too which I admired devoutly." The remark about the "quasi-Dostoievskian note" now seems doubtful, but Dell showed a rare perspicacity in announcing Anderson as an important new writer.

In 1913 Anderson sent *Windy* to Alfred Harcourt, then an editor at Henry Holt & Co., who accepted it on condition that changes be made in its clumsy style. Anderson agreed, but when he saw the proposed changes he angrily withdrew his book. In the fall of 1913, when Dell left to become an editor of *The Masses*, he took *Windy* to New York, hoping to find a publisher for it. The mere fact that Dell was ready to put himself to such trouble was a sign that Anderson had finally entered, as he had so long hoped to, the literary world.

Sherwood Anderson was particularly fortunate that he arrived in Chicago shortly before that city's "literary renaissance" reached its brief climax. More than most of the other mid-American writers to whom the Chicago Bohemia seemed or was soon to seem a magnet of hope, he needed the stimulus of literary talk and the bolstering of literary groups. His years in Chicago, in which for the first time he had the "feeling of brotherhood and sisterhood with men and women whose interests were my own," always seemed to him "the gayest and happiest I have ever known." The seriousness, the unconventionality and the camaraderie for which he had yearned, he now found in Bohemia.

Chicago already had a rather thin *avant-garde* tradition, first notably manifested in the 1890's when two intelligent Harvard graduates formed the publishing house of Stone & Kimball. Besides issuing Shaw, Ibsen, Yeats, and Verlaine, the firm sponsored *The Chapbook*, a little magazine that featured translations of the French Symbolists. That its American contributors, headed by Hamlin Garland and Joaquin Miller, seem somewhat shabby by comparison, was hardly Stone & Kimball's fault. For this was a dreary moment in American writing, when even the quite bold *Chapbook* printed the verses of Edmund Clarence Stedman and Ella Wheeler Wilcox, and when Chicago's literary leader was Henry B. Fuller, whose novels ran to mild realism or mild decadence.

Chicago literary life was frankly derivative; the best things in *The Chapbook* came from France and England, its native writers made no serious effort to surmount the tone of gentility, and even such realists as Garland, Herrick, and Fuller were not likely to shock any but the most starched Victorian minds. It was only in 1911, when Francis Hackett became editor of the *Friday Literary Review*, a weekly supplement of the *Chicago Evening Post*, that sustained voices began to call for both an indigenous realism and an acceptance of the best in contemporary European writing.

During the next several years, under the successive editorship of Hackett, Floyd Dell, and Lucian Cary, the *Friday Review* became a first-rate literary paper. To both its youthful contributors and its regular readers, the *Fri-*

day Review gave literary leadership, calling for a reformation in American writing and teaching the uninitiated to discern the genuinely "new note." The paper printed articles on such Europeans as Strindberg, Shaw, Schnitzler, Sudermann, D'Annunzio; it ran regular literary letters from Paris, London and New York; it did not hesitate to offer serious 4,000-word essays on Bergson's *Creative Evolution* and Frazer's *Golden Bough*; it ripped into philistines like William Lyon Phelps with an antiseptic ferocity still rare in newspaper reviewing; it slyly disparaged *Jean-Christophe* and gently deflated Masefield's reputation; it mocked such relics of gentility as F. Marion Crawford—but above everything else it fought the one literary battle of its day that involved risk and commitment: it championed the new realists. Dreiser became its rallying call, as indeed in 1912 he had to be for anyone seriously concerned with a vital American literature.

Floyd Dell, Dreiser's most fervent though not uncritical champion, was the intellectual guide for the *Friday Review*; his articles were lucid, informed, and, for a man still in his early twenties, remarkably sympathetic. He anticipated many of the major themes of subsequent American criticism; in a review of Gorky's *Lower Depths* he wrote: "In being a free people we suffer a certain disadvantage. We cannot understand the seriousness with which those who are less free take the process of thinking." This, as much else like it, is well said; yet Dell never quite managed the leap from superior reviewing to serious criticism. His writing clarified and entertained, but it seldom undercut to that ultimate insight which alone is the justification of criticism. His difficulty was due far less to the confinements of journalism than to the fact that he wrote at a time when there was no active and nourishing cultural environment that could guide, deepen, and sometimes clip his splendid enthusiasms. Dell, and the *Friday Review* with him, may now seem to have had more bounce than weight, but this was a limitation inevitable at a time when a few people in Chicago were trying hurriedly to create a culture on the cuff.

It is a limitation that appears more important in retrospect than it could possibly have in 1912, when all that mattered was that new and plausible claims to genius were being entered each day. In 1912 Harriet Monroe started *Poetry: A Magazine of Verse*, Carl Sandburg was working as a socialist newspaperman and writing verses on the side, Maurice Browne opened his 99-seat Little Theatre, Vachel Lindsay wrote "General William Booth Enters into Heaven," and the Irish Players were rapturously received in Chicago. Within a few years *Poetry* printed some of the earliest poems of Lindsay, Pound, Sandburg, Lawrence, Aldington, Stevens, Marianne Moore, and Eliot. After presenting plays by Yeats and Schnitzler, the Little Theatre plunged into Gilbert Murray's translation of *The Trojan Women*. The Post-Impressionist show came to Chicago, and Sherwood and Karl Anderson went day after day to stare at the astonishing pictures by Cézanne, Van Gogh, and Gauguin. And in early 1914 Margaret Anderson began her erratic, insistently unconventional *Little Review*, in which she anticipated the "little magazine" tone of the 1920's.

What seemed to the Chicago writers a sectional spurt of creative activity was related to a cultural outburst in Europe during the second decade of the century. Picasso, Stravinsky, Joyce, Matisse, Lawrence—these names could not yet mean much in Chicago and their achievements could hardly be understood or measured. But the mere fact that the Chicago intellectuals heard occasional reports of Europe's cultural revolution strengthened their hopes for boldness and originality, and above all spurred their willingness to take chances.

Though the "Chicago Renaissance," as its participants never let themselves forget, was centered in a big city, it can best be understood against the backdrop of the Midwestern small towns from which most of its young writers came. Dell came from Davenport, Iowa; Hecht from Racine, Wisconsin; Sandburg from Galesburg, Illinois; Masters from Garnett, Kansas. They had fled the drab towns where each had felt himself isolated and misunderstood, and they had come to the city large with inchoate ambitions, hungry for an exchange of hopes, ideas, and flattery, and expecting to find jobs at least somewhat related to their intellectual goals. Over their consciousness the town hung like a weight of sodden and nostalgic hatred, and try as they might to polish themselves against Chicago, New York, and Paris, they would remain townsmen to the end of their days: Sandburg, Anderson, perhaps even the Ezra Pound who studied Chinese.

The Midwestern towns, after several generations of consuming work, were now beginning to win some of that security and leisure which is a prerequisite to any cultural response. The towns, in truth, were barren enough, impoverished by the old rural harshness and the new industrial crudity, but that they were mere deserts of philistinism is a legend disproved by the very existence of the writers who first advanced it. The towns had been greatly stirred during the last two decades of the 19th

and the first decade of the 20th century; the rebellion
of Populism, the educative impulse so often behind the
formation of Socialist locals, the lecture tours of suffra-
gists, atheists, and radicals had all brought moods of self-
conscious dissatisfaction. No doubt, these moods actively
infected only small minorities, but it was necessary for a
few townsmen to apprehend the barrenness of their lives
and to begin searching for some tokens of meaning and
grace before there could arise young men able to trans-
mute this search into the matter of art. It was, however,
the fate of the towns that they would be repudiated precisely at the moment a few of their young people began to
simmer with cultural ambition, for the first consequence
of self-consciousness is almost always the rejection of the
milieu which formed it.

Yet even the most insistently sophisticated of the Chicago writers remained small-townmen in many ways.
That, paradoxically, was why they could so readily accept
Chicago, why Sandburg could so rapturously embrace the
"City of the Big Shoulders," and Anderson so loudly
chant its wonders: "You know my city—Chicago trium-
phant; factories and marts and roar of machines—horri-
ble, terrible, ugly and brutal." No one who had actually
lived his life in the city was likely to take so romantic a
view of it, could so eagerly pounce on it for "material."

The Chicago writers remained small-townmen in another and more fundamental sense. When they found
themselves lonely in the city, as it was inevitable that
they would, they began to recreate the town, not in the
shape of its reality, but in the image of those ideal com-
munities for which they had yearned during their original town loneliness. The Bohemias, the Greenwich Vil-

lages are always the work of young writers and artists who, on the margin or in the interstices of the city, come together to recover the intimacy of the town while hoping to realize the freedom they had expected to find in the city. What they had come to find they would, in its absence, improvise; and for a little while believe it really there, independent of their will or buttress. Like Archibald Higbie of Spoon River, where "there was no culture," they would, "pray for another/ Birth in the world, with all of Spoon River/ Rooted out of my soul." When a young poetess like Eunice Tietjens first arrived in Chicago, she was invited to a poetry evening at the Dells' and later that night she "walked on air, like one warm with champagne, though I had had no alcohol except of the spirit." She could hardly have known that most of the others at that poetry evening had themselves only recently "walked on air," and that she was meeting not a sustaining new world but a multiple image, as it were, of herself.

What these young people wanted most of all was fraternity, a center in which they could warm and reassure each other, in which they could shake off the American curse of loneliness. How terrifying that loneliness could seem, how much an inescapable part of the American experience, is the burden of Edgar Lee Masters's lugubrious but moving autobiography *Across Spoon River:*

> All my life I have endured loneliness. . . . As a boy on the Masters farm the silence of the prairie had seemed to me to be the silence of my own heart. And in the stillness of the evenings when the sun set beyond the farthest farmhouses I walked about the pastures

. . . with something choking in my breast, with a longing I could not understand.

With an exasperated futility Masters was to struggle to articulate and then transcend "the silence of my own heart"; his autobiography is an essential document for the study of the American writer's alienation from his formative milieu. But even so naturally gregarious a being as Sherwood Anderson would reach, by indirection, conclusions similar to those of Masters:

> There was in us, I am sure, something of the fervor that must have taken hold of those earlier Americans who had attempted to found communistic communities. We were, in our own minds, a little band of soldiers who were going to free life (first of all, to be sure, our own lives) from certain bonds.
>
> No, it wasn't exactly free love we wanted. I doubt that there was with us any more giving way to the simple urge to sex than among the advertising and business men among whom I worked. . . . Indeed sex was to be given a new dignity. . . .
>
> I think we wanted to reveal something, bring something back. Later my own observation of life in small Middle-Western towns as boy and young man was to lead to the writing of my *Winesburg*.

At first reading there seems no logical relation in this passage between its last sentence and those preceding it, but there is a deep, perhaps unwitting rightness to the movement of Anderson's memory. For he is really saying that the great value of the Chicago experience was that it stimulated and released him for *Winesburg*, his most significant work; his flight to Bohemia was a condition for his creative recovery of the town. And what was the dominating subject of *Winesburg*, as of *Spoon River* before it, if not the town-loneliness which the Chicago writers had sought to escape?

In the immediate present, however, it seemed as if this loneliness might finally be discarded. Particularly for a man like Anderson, in whom receptiveness to new experience became a kind of psychic strut, the Chicago Bohemia was completely absorbing and exhilarating. Being gifted at social adaptation he soon found himself accepted in literary circles, of which the most important was one that had centered in Floyd Dell and, after Dell's departure to New York, continued to gather in ramshackle stores on the South Side's 57th Street. In those dank hutches, built in 1892 for the World's Fair but now serving as studios for writers and artists, Anderson became friendly with such young writers as Ben Hecht, George Cram Cook, Arthur D. Ficke, Lucian Cary, Ernestine Evans, and Robert Morss Lovett.

Sometimes Theodore Dreiser would visit 57th Street. To the young writers, even those sophisticated enough to consider his work "crude," Dreiser seemed a literary pioneer: he had liberated American writing from gentility and restored to it the actuality of life—actuality then being a category highly valued in literary discussion. And when Dreiser praised a bit of *Windy McPherson's Son* at a 57th Street party, it was a prized moment for Anderson, one which helped assuage his ineradicable uncertainty about the value of his work.

Many of the members of this loosely bound group were, like Dell, newspaper reporters. Though at least several were well read in European literature and considered it their responsibility to inform Chicago readers of the European cultural news, their main interest was in the creation of an American literature that would deserve the thunder of their favorite adjectives: real, fearless, vital. They felt warm ties with the contemporary European realists, but they worked on the assumption that in America there was no cultural tradition either valuable or accessible. Though they were serious, admirably serious, they suspected the highbrows, for the highbrows were not sufficiently *real:* highbrows were academic or thin-blooded or, as Hecht was later to say, wrote about Art as if it were their dead grandmother.

Perhaps then Anderson was the real thing. Under the endlessly sympathetic guidance of Margery Curry, a young reporter who had been Dell's wife and was now the group's social center, Anderson began to assume, even before his publication, a position of quasi-superiority. The others might feel intellectually beyond him, they had certainly read more books than he; but he had lived and suffered more than they, and—here was the miracle!—in middle age had extricated himself from the mire of philistinism. Anderson, who assumed literary roles partly out of guile but mainly because he found an ironic pleasure in satisfying the naïve expectations of his sophisticated friends, now became the folk-poet who, from the bowels of the people's wisdom and experience, would bring forth a new truth. The others sometimes laughed at him, but they were nonetheless impressed, and the more Bohemian and distant from common life they were, the more they were impressed. It was no accident that of all Anderson's Chicago friends Ben Hecht was to give his early books the most laudatory reviews.

What would have surprised those friends was Anderson's inner uncertainty, his need to hoard slights. Many years later, in reviewing Anderson's *Memoirs*, Floyd Dell was to note: "We certainly never guessed that, underneath his gaiety, he was full of doubts, fears and dark suspicions. He seems to have been sure that other people thought he was a fool for trying to write. And what Sherwood imagined that you thought was to him exactly as if you really said it." Yet how could his friends know how difficult it was for him to believe in himself as a writer? How could they know how galling it was to hear young snips talk learnedly about authors whom one had never read or perhaps heard of?

The symptoms of Anderson's insecurity were numerous. Though the Bohemian groups welcomed him, he kept a certain distance from them, quite by deliberate intent. To break himself of his businessman's nervously rapid speech, as well as to develop a touch of picturesqueness, he cultivated a slow, slightly "southern" drawl. (If he could fabricate a southern ancestry, he might as well improvise an accompanying accent.) Though he could now see how pathetic were the literary ambitions of his advertising friends, he maintained close relations with them, not merely out of personal loyalty but because he needed their soothing admiration. For similar reasons he enjoyed living in 1915 with "the little children of the arts," a group of penniless young writers and artists who respected him as their experienced senior. And when Margaret Anderson founded her *Little Review*, he instinctively gravitated toward it, for there neither ideas nor knowledge counted, only originality.

What saved Anderson in these years was the pervasive freshness and naïveté of the circles in which he lived, and his genuine capacity for personal pleasure which often enabled him to push aside his anxieties. He loved to sit in Schlogel's Restaurant, the center of the literary newspapermen, and listen to Hecht unravel gaudy strings of adjectives, Harry Hansen lecture on German literature, Burton Rascoe cuss out the arid Professors. When Anderson met someone whom he found sympathetic, he could relax into easy and charming conversation. To Alfred Kreymborg, then equally a romanticist in temperament, Anderson's "fine head of auburn hair, large luminous eyes, stocky physique and distinguished gestures gave the impression that life sat well on him. He talked with remarkable ease, the more so as the topic . . . was the relation between man and woman, a topic Sherwood approached with tender simplicity. . . . He had the air of a man on the threshold of experience"—as, indeed, he was to have all his life.

To each of the circles in which he mingled Anderson seemed a somewhat different personality. To the 57th Street group he seemed the middle-class American who had lifted himself out of a poisonous environment; to the *Little Review* circle, a delightfully innocent primitive— a misapprehension for which the magazine was properly punished by becoming the receptacle for his worst writing; and to his advertising friends, a man who would soon escape the drudgery of copy-writing. Little wonder then that Anderson preferred to keep somewhat separate his various circles of friends; had they persistently overlapped, he would have been dizzied by the blur of his several images of himself.

Nowhere did he so enjoy himself as in the boarding-house at 735 Cass Street where he was the dean of "the little children of the arts." Here, free of competitive pressures, he could release his natural high spirits and rich sense of play. At night he would walk on Cass Street with a huge brass ring hooked to his ear, and chortle over the attention he aroused. When his friend Tennessee Mitchell took him to the opera, he returned to tell the "little children of the arts" that the music left him indifferent but that the costumes were marvelous—"in those days," he said, men knew how to dress. In his room his bed was raised high so that while lying in it he could have a full view of the Chicago he loved to romanticize. And when he wrote on his huge table, he would sometimes light candles to the gods of inspiration—an act of devotion, half play and half serious, elicited perhaps by his continuing amazement at having become a writer at all.

Such behavior by a man in his late thirties, a father of three children and only recently a paint manufacturer, was possible because the life of Bohemian Chicago was itself so innocent and self-indulgent. A few of the writers, like Masters, had been crippled by their struggle for expression and their hunger for companionship, but most of them were in the enviable position of being able to think of themselves with unqualified hope. They were ready to take chances with their futures, and it was their fortune that taking chances hardly seemed a risk.

That the "Chicago Renaissance" felt no intolerable press of idea or ideology was a cause of its evanescent happiness, as later of its final failure. The sense of Europe which was to disturb American literary life in the 1920's did not yet exist in the Chicago of 1912-16. Europe was then a source from which one could, without jeopardy or involvement, draw cultural nourishment, or it was a place of vaguely impinging troubles—but hardly the doom it later seemed. Equally absent was the social rebelliousness and guilt that was to rake American intellectual life in the 1930's. There were, to be sure, such socialists as Floyd Dell, but when Sinclair Lewis called Dell a faun on the barricades he was rather close to the truth. Most of the Chicago writers who cared about socialism at all thought of it merely as the terminus of a joyous and visible democratic expansion. And whatever else it was, socialism was certainly no cause for worry.

It was a moment in American intellectual life, soon to be ended, when the young writer could, without too immediate harm, resist the idea of a life of ideas. Socialism was bland, religion passé, Freudianism a not yet influential murmur from the East, though by 1913 a psychoanalytical primer had been reviewed in the *Friday Review* and the intellectuals had begun to play games based on word associations and memory lapses. As long as freedom seemed indefinitely expansible and aspiration unlimited, ideas could hardly press the young writer too seriously.

In Margaret Anderson the period found its consummate expression. After abandoning her middle-class parents, she lived in the Chicago Y.W.C.A., worked as a book reviewer for a church paper, and in 1914 started the *Little Review* with almost no money and rather less policy. Though she possessed only one blouse she was untroubled by that paralyzing need for security which was to afflict writers of later generations. When she had no money for rent or printer's bills, she moved into a tent on the North Shore, where she spent six months editing the *Little Review* and washing the blouse nightly in Lake

Michigan. Like a chain of ceaselessly sputtering firecrackers, her articles hailed the wonders of the world as she discovered them each month: the wonders of the Machine Age, the wonders of anarchism, the wonders of the Nietzschean Superman. In an editorial note she announced the magazine's policy to be "A Will to Splendor in Life," a phrase that aptly suggested both her purpose and the Chicago tone.

Even in the more sedate office of *Poetry*, where Harriet Monroe presided like a slightly misplaced schoolteacher, this tone triumphed. Eunice Tietjens, who was *Poetry's* assistant editor for a year, has recalled a startling visit from Vachel Lindsay during which he enlisted the editors as chorus for a new poem. "I can still see little Harriet Monroe, her cheeks quite pink with excitement, and big myself . . . representing King Solomon's four hundred wives and dutifully chanting 'We are the wives' while Vachel took our hands in turn and with a beautiful old-world courtesy led us through the mazes of a sort of dance he had devised for the purpose. At such times the office became a fairy world." Whoever would measure the distance between this atmosphere and that of several decades later need only try to imagine a similar scene at the office of one of our literary quarterlies.

To Sherwood Anderson this Chicago tone was something to enjoy and play with, though his shrewdness prevented him from taking it too seriously. When Tennessee Mitchell started a class in the modern dance, Anderson, his bulky body draped in a white sheet, tried cheerfully to follow her choreographic directions. When "Floyd Dell and I talked of Pater and of living with the hard gemlike flame," Margaret Anderson has recalled, "Sherwood

Anderson used to listen to us in a certain amazement (resembling fear) and indicating clearly that nothing would induce him into such fancy realms. . . . He didn't talk ideas—he told stories." The suggestion that Anderson felt toward the intellectuals something like fear is very acute, but it is doubtful that he was really as amazed as he led them to believe. Whether or not he had heard of Pater, he knew about the hard gem-like flame; he had been looking for it these past ten years.

That flame, it seemed to the Chicago writers, might be found in two literary directions: the search for personal and creative freedom, and the attempt to nurture a distinct Midwestern literary consciousness. Exactly what freedom meant to them, few of the Chicago writers bothered seriously to inquire; they were too busy hunting for it. As late as 1930 Margaret Anderson, who was forever to echo her past with unabashed fidelity, could write: "I am no man's wife, no man's delightful mistress, and I will never, never be a mother." Such overwhelming proclamations were quite in the spirit of a time in which it seemed that freedom meant simply escape from the conventional town and conventional family, an indiscriminate enthusiasm for the native and the novel, and a rather disastrous impatience with close thought in literary discussion or anywhere else. To the young writers it seemed reasonable to suppose that if one's desire for freedom were sufficiently intense freedom could sooner or later be had, and that if a *real* American culture would ever arise it would come only from the "free spirits" of the Midwest. For a few years this atmosphere did stimulate some lively writing; with so much energy and talent at hand almost any ideas would have been momentarily usable. But few of the Chicago writers were able to grow beyond the stage of irrupted enthusiasm; most of them did their best work immediately after initial publication. That they were short-breathed and yet tried to run cross-country was their common tragedy.

Even as an image of utopia, the freedom these writers sought was rapidly becoming an anachronism, for it was a freedom related to a level of social development the Midwest had already outgrown. It is an historical curiosity that in the Chicago Bohemia of 1912-15 the populist values of 19th-century mid-America received such thorough, but already obsolete, expression and criticism—obsolete because the criticism, no matter how violent, never transcended the limits of the expression.

Often enough, what the young Chicago writer had in mind was simply a wish for a brilliant career, to escape from the town to Chicago and then to New York. In moments of social fluidity it is easy enough to identify one's ambitions with a larger urge toward freedom: the shawl of egotism covers both. But once most of the Chicago writers gained a bit of fame, and with it enough security to see themselves in perspective, they began to realize how narrow and paltry had been their conception of freedom. In his autobiography Masters lacerated himself on his memories of repeated erotic experiences, each more dismal than the other, and none leading to emotional release or fulfillment. Floyd Dell, in his autobiographical novel *The Briary Bush*, swung a full circle from Bohemianism to a dreary bourgeois conventionality: his hero, after concluding that freedom was more to be feared than sought, decides to remake his life by building a house in the country. Which, as it happened, was what most of the Chicago writers eventually did. Only Anderson, in his lifelong wanderings through the country, remained loyal to the dream of freedom—personal, ultimate, and unrelated to social limits; it was his wistful clinging to that dream in all its dignity and absurdity and pathos that made his writing so unique an American expression.

Somewhat like the quest for freedom, the attempt to construct an indigenous Midwestern literature was the result of an inadequate and belated consciousness. What the Chicago writers took to be the first rude step to a sectional literature was actually the last outburst of Midwestern consciousness, and as such deserved every possible honor except the belief that it had a future. The notion that the Midwestern writers, following Dreiser, would at last penetrate to the reality of American life was insupportable for several reasons: the era when sectional differences were still significant was fast dying, the Midwestern school required from its adherents a terribly impoverished reading of American literary history, and consequently the perception of reality held by these writers was itself insufficient. When so sentimental an eastern writer as Alfred Kreymborg came to Chicago, he found the city "the broad-shouldered titan he had been looking for to lead the nation out of the craven past. . . . Here was no dependence on New York and *via* New York, an abject prostration to Europe. . . ." This is the language of Midwestern braggadocio, borrowed from those who never bothered to ask whether the Chicago writers might not have learned from the despised 19th-century New Englanders something about the resources of the English language, whether Anderson might not have learned from the Hawthorne and the James he scorned something about the complexities of human intercourse. Was, after all, the American past exhausted by that one fearful adjective: Puritan? In their hearts the shrewder Midwestern writers, and none more than Anderson, knew that their backgrounds were unequal to their ambitions, that they were trapped in the Midwest's dead-end as a sectional culture. Their only recourse was to believe that tradition was a mere burden and that they themselves, their verse freed and their freedom incessantly celebrated, would create by fiat the background they did not have.

At the moment this belief seemed fruitful if only because there was a powerful enemy against whom to battle: the entrenched spokesmen of literary sentimentalism and gentility. But by judging themselves only or largely in relation to this immediate enemy, the Chicago writers committed a fatal self-indulgence: failing to bring into play the best available standards, they transformed their limitations into a program. Throughout his life Anderson was to preach the need for freeing the short story from O. Henry's conventional plot formulae—which was true enough, but which soon began to seem too easy and even irrelevant.

What it came to in the end was that the "Chicago Renaissance" had a peculiarly inadequate vision of itself. No period can be seen in full perspective by its participants, but in few periods of American literary history have writers been so taken at their own valuation. The Chicago writers needed most of all severe, objective, and serious criticism; instead, as Kreymborg cheerfully observed, they got "log-rolling." The least that criticism can do for its time is to puncture complacency, but while Hecht and Rascoe were ready to denounce one and all in the outer darkness, they were beatifically lyrical about the Chicago writers. There was plenty of talent in Chicago; what was lacking was a serious view of the human situation, a comprehension of the immediate historical moment, a willingness to judge work by the most severe standards. Most of the Chicago writers never emerged from their regional *Sturm und Drang,* never realized that a serious writer must move beyond the celebration of his escape from the world's boredom and ugliness.

This innocent egotism marked the ultimate failure of the Chicago school. To her dying day Harriet Monroe believed that free verse and imagism were the last word in modern poetry, that in a magazine which had published Eliot, Lawrence, and Pound "perhaps the most gifted and original poet we ever printed" was Lindsay. And the final debacle of too many Chicago writers, particularly the critics, was that, like Mencken somewhat later, they substituted a violent assertion of personality for tact, judgment, and knowledge.

In their willingness to replace thought with a program of emotion, the Chicago writers fatally restricted their rendering of or relation to human experience. Much of their failure is explained in Eunice Tietjens's observation that Margaret Anderson had "a kind of savage scorn of everything she did not understand." That savage scorn came through in Dell's later novels, in Hecht's blatant articles, in Rascoe's professor-baiting, and in Anderson's rather thoughtless complaints about his critics.

Fortunately for Anderson, however, the limiting effects of the Chicago period did not appear in his work until the middle 1920's, by which time he had completed his best work. It is an ironic comment on the workings of cultural influence that the milieu whose "sophisticated" values contributed to the failure of his last books should have yet released his talents for such achievements as *Winesburg, Ohio* and *The Triumph of the Egg.*

In 1916 Anderson published the novel *Windy Mc-Pherson's Son* which he had written in Elyria, as well as several of the *Winesburg* sketches. Floyd Dell had unsuccessfully canvassed the New York publishers with *Windy*, and as a last hope had sent it to England where it was accepted by John Lane. Issued simultaneously in England and the United States, *Windy* roused the Chicago writers to enthusiastic excess, Hecht reviewing it as a "literary miracle" and Dell as the work of "a mind full of beautiful, intense and perilous emotions."

Had they been writing only of the book's opening chapters, their praise might almost have been justified, for few American first novels begin as well as *Windy* and demonstrate so distinct a command of a new subject matter. Anderson's vision of the small town was that of a place where people haphazardly enter into social relations that can yield no personal values. Since the society portrayed in *Windy* is still socially fluid, the townspeople are not severely bound by status; their problem is rather that they have no principle about which to order their lives, they are scattered human units.

This condition is probably unavoidable in a raw society, and Caxton, Iowa, the town in which the novel's initial action occurs, is as raw as Anderson's prose. Most of its more conscious residents intermittently grope for a sense of identity, but the town, like the civilization it congeals, can offer no touchstone against which to try identity. In an unconsciously right adaptation to his subject matter, which is the paradox of a society simultaneously unformed and atrophied, Anderson's writing is neither naturalistic nor even realistic; individual phrases and sentences are quite conventional but the vision behind them is grotesque and extravagant. As is always true of Anderson's best writing, he employs grotesque perceptions most effectively when his material is heavily freighted with a sense of reality.

In *Windy* that reality is the press of childhood memory releasing an intimate and authentic emotion, father-hatred. Windy McPherson, "a confirmed liar and blusterer," is a vicious re-creation of Anderson's own father, vividly dominating the book's early pages and not sweetened by that dubious "understanding" which Anderson was later to offer his father's memory. Windy is not a "rounded" character; neither is Sam McPherson, the boy driven by ambition as a response to his father's shiftlessness; nor Mike McCarthy, the atheist unbalanced by his isolation; nor John Telfer, the bleary intellectual who rejects the town yet is its official spokesman; they are rather bold, quickly drawn social caricatures, animated by Anderson's welling memory.

The most effective episode in the novel shows Windy riding a white horse at a Caxton Fourth of July celebration, so haughty and fine that he arouses pride even in his scornful son. Rising in his saddle Windy begins to blow his bugle, but the result, of course, is a fiasco: he cannot play the instrument, the crowd laughs itself into tears, and Windy is left bewildered: "He had heard the thing a thousand times and had it clearly in his mind; with all his heart he wanted it to roll forth and could

picture the street ringing with it and the applause of
the people; the thing, he felt, was in him, and it was only
a fatal blunder in nature that it did not come out at the
flaring end of the bugle." Sam, humiliated, runs off to the
woods and cries out: "You may laugh at that fool Windy,
but you shall never laugh at Sam McPherson."

Both for its conscious charge that the father is an empty
braggart and its unconscious insinuation of impotence
(that "fatal blunder in nature"), the episode is a cruel ret-
ribution. But in the book's context Sam's cruelty does not
seem excessive, for it is not merely an act of filial repudia-
tion but also a rejection of that stretch of the American
past of which Windy is a symbolic caricature. The episode
thereby has a ring of almost mythic American authenticity, it locates an area of American experience as surely as
Babbitt's ritual of early morning rising or Drouet's flirta-
tion with Sister Carrie on the train to Chicago.

Windy McPherson's Son collapses, however, at precisely its most daring and what might have been its most
powerful moment: Sam's attempt to kill his father. In the
hands of a dramatic novelist, the open climax of the parri-
cidal wish could have resulted in a sustained and terrible
piece of writing, but Anderson's treatment is conspicuously unemphatic. Perhaps this failure is due to an unconscious revulsion from what he has at last dared say
about his father, perhaps to a more pervasive incapacity
for rendering dramatic conflict, but whatever the reason it
marks the point at which *Windy* ceases to engage the serious reader.

The last two-thirds of the novel is a shoddy affair, its
fumbling aggravated by Anderson's painful effort to
achieve sophistication. Sam McPherson leaves his home

for Chicago, marries his boss's daughter, rises rapidly to wealth, finds himself dissatisfied with his business life and childless marriage, and then abandons business and wife to wander through the country seeking a new meaning by which to live. This tale is partly a reworking of the American success fable trimmed with the sentimentalities of magazine fiction, partly a daydream version of Anderson's own career. *Windy* also has that curiously sexless quality of those of Anderson's later novels which have been read as sex-centered: Sam's two women are a crippled intellectual and a high-toned, probably frigid wife who evades sexual intimacy on her marriage night and repeatedly fails to bear live children. It would be hazardous and perhaps presumptuous to relate this aspect of the novel directly to Anderson's personal experience, but it does not seem too far-fetched to assume, in view of the breakdown that followed a few years after he wrote it, that the problem of sexual fulfillment did harass him during his Elyria years.

After deciding that "American men and women have not learned to be clean and noble and natural, like their forests and their wide, clean plains," Sam McPherson returns to his wife, bringing with him three neglected children he has picked up during his travels. "Man," he declares, "wants children—not his own children—any children." Such a conclusion, implying that the search for truth rightly leads to intimate love, might seem plausible if tactfully controlled by an experienced writer. In *Windy*, however, it is rather ridiculous, if only because it is a gesture abruptly appended to a novel that has been insisting continuously on the unavoidability of isolation.

Windy is clearly the work of a writer who has yet to

make his peace with the English language. Its continuity is repeatedly broken by Anderson's lumbering reflections; the proportion of abstract narrative to immediate representation is much too high; and the writing itself represents an unhappy fusion of the colloquial with what passes for elegant language among businessmen. (Of one Caxton citizen Anderson remarks: "His *sang froid* had returned to him.") Nor does Anderson display unusual descriptive powers: nothing in *Windy's* Chicago compares with Dreiser's punctilious observations of the city's hotel and factory life.

Had Anderson directed his major energies to becoming a social novelist, *Windy* would be remembered, if at all, as a dreary portent of failure. As it is, the first 75 pages of the novel constitute not only a successful fragment but, with regard to both tone and subject matter, a necessary prelude to the achievement of *Winesburg*. And in its entirety the novel is still a moving instance of an American's effort to lift himself from the mire of inarticulation to the ambiance of art.

It is a coincidence, yet an apposite one, that simultaneously with his publication of a novel so thoroughly dependent on childhood memories and small-town atmospheres, Anderson embarked on the one major experience of his life that might conceivably be called Bohemian. In August 1916, a year after his first wife had divorced him, Anderson married Tennessee Mitchell, a music teacher who frequented the Chicago Bohemia. Faithful to the fashionable notions of the day, they maintained separate apartments for most of their marriage, an arrangement that satisfied Anderson's wish to be free of personal responsibilities.

At the age of 17 Tennessee Mitchell, who had been named after Tennessee Claflin, a 19th-century suffragist, left her home in Jackson, Michigan and came to Chicago. Extremely poor, she found work as a piano tuner (she had perfect pitch) and then rose to teaching music and rhythmic dancing to the children of Chicago's "Gold Coast" families. To her the city represented the possibility of personal and cultural growth; she worked hard, read considerably, listened carefully, and devoted herself to self-cultivation with the earnestness of a provincial schoolteacher intent on sucking cosmopolitan culture dry. Both as woman and as worker she aggressively asserted her independence, and only later, when for her it was too late, did she realize the insufficiency of her code. In almost all of the Chicago intellectuals, as well as those of Anderson's New York friends who later met her, she aroused a rather begrudging and uneasy admiration. In her seeming self-assurance, her satiric yet not unkind wit, her readiness to live out her commitment, she was the typical "New Woman." Tennessee was not good-looking: she was tall and gawky, coarse-featured, large-boned, and almost asexual to the eye, suggesting something of the starkness of the frontier of which she was a not too distant descendant. Though after her marriage she began to assume the airs of a grand lady, she could not suppress her typically American concern with getting ahead, even if only in the little world in which she had chosen to live.

Like all of Anderson's wives, she now seems to have

been related to a distinct phase of his experience, in this instance that period after his conventional first marriage when he yearned for a bold and free style of life. For a time Tennessee was ready to relieve him of many of his personal responsibilities, since leadership came naturally to her and up to a point Anderson was pleased to be led. She championed his career and propped his confidence; she heralded the life of the "free spirit" and yet assuaged his ego by remaining conventionally faithful to him. What she would demand in return she did not yet know.

In one of Anderson's unpublished novels, *Mary Cochran*, the heroine seems remarkably similar to Tennessee. An early version of this novel was written in Elyria, but Anderson rewrote it in 1919 and may, by then, have used Tennessee as a model for Mary Cochran's experience in Chicago. Like Tennessee, Mary comes to the big city to mold a life of her own: she is earnest, lonely, hawklike in her eagerness to swallow experience. Like Tennessee, she "was not a licentious woman. . . . She was a woman whose place in life it was to do some one piece of work honestly and well." And the words Mary uses in a moment of rebelliousness might well be Tennessee's: "I shall not feel that I have something to sell for which I must get a roof over my head and a man to work for me. I shall have my man but I shall choose him boldly and without fear." These lines suggest Tennessee all the more strongly when it is known that she was the one who, in her relations with Anderson, pressed boldly for marriage.

Quite appropriately, their marriage took place at a camp near Lake Chateaugay in upstate New York, where intellectuals came to take the "rhythms." On their honeymoon the Andersons visited Cornelia Anderson in the

Indiana town where she worked as a teacher, and Cornelia and Tennessee, with insistent tolerance, renewed a friendship that had begun in 1914. Tennessee began to assume some of Anderson's responsibilities for raising the children, and in the summer of 1917 she arranged that Cornelia, the three children, Anderson, and she go, one might almost say *en famille*, to Lake Chateaugay. This, too, was the new freedom.

Anderson's contract with John Lane had given the publisher option rights to his next three books. Since he had several book-length manuscripts at hand, Anderson could now begin to publish at the rate of one book a year. In 1917, accordingly, Lane brought out *Marching Men*, which Anderson had written in Elyria.

In *Marching Men*, Anderson took a step farther on the path of discontent. *Marching Men* shows no confidence in the intentions of enlightened businessmen, but rather urges the more violent view that the nation can be righted only by a charismatic leader who will whip the masses into revolt. Like *Windy*, it begins as a crude *Entwicklungsroman*: Beaut McGregor, a powerful gawky boy, revolts against the passivity of Coal Creek, a Pennsylvania mining town. Though revering the memory of his father, a martyred miner, he despises the miners *en masse*, somewhat like a Lawrencian hero, for their drab acceptance of misery. When he leaves Coal Creek to make his fortune in Chicago, he looks back "full of hate . . . he might have wished that all of the people of the town had but one head so that he might cut it off. . . ." But, if we are to believe Anderson, McGregor's misanthropic feeling toward the miners is dissolved when he returns to

Coal Creek to watch them form a spontaneous parade of honor at his mother's funeral. Like all of Anderson's heroes, McGregor experiences a moment of intense perception which changes the entire course of his life: ". . . he had of a sudden one of those strange awakenings . . . he tried vainly to get back his old satisfying hate of the town and the miners but it would not come . . . they like himself were marching up out of the smoke and the little squalid houses, away from the shores of the blood-red river into something new." The transformed McGregor is to be the people's liberator.

In Chicago he becomes the leader of a movement known as the "marching men," a group of workers united in dumb brotherhood to find "the secret of order in the midst of this disorder." The world, cries McGregor, "should become a great camp. . . . Why should some men not begin the organization of a new army? If there are men who do not understand what is meant let them be knocked down."

When McGregor is asked the destination of his marching men, he answers, apparently to Anderson's satisfaction, in a free-verse leaflet:

> They ask us what we mean.
> Well, here is our answer.
> We mean to go on marching . . .
> We will not talk nor listen to talk. . . .

At a vast Labor Day parade McGregor tells his followers that if one of them "whines or complains or stands upon a box throwing words about, knock him down and keep marching." True to his monomaniacal creed, McGregor beats a tired follower and warns him, "This is no time for words." At the novel's end the movement collapses for reasons that are never clear, perhaps because Anderson hadn't the faintest notion of what to do with it. But McGregor is in no way diminished or disparaged as a popular leader, and even the capitalist responsible for his defeat wonders whether McGregor was not right after all.

It is impossible to read this novel today without a shudder, for history has lent Anderson's marching men a significance he could hardly have intended. Yet the novel has been charitably ignored or misconstrued by almost all of Anderson's critics, whether because they have not read it or read it with increasing embarrassment one does not know. When it first appeared in 1917, Francis Hackett reviewed it in the *New Republic* as "a graphic proletarian novel," and the socialist *Liberator*, which should have known better, called it "a novel of ideas." In an essay written in the 1920's, the radical critic V. F. Calverton described *Marching Men* as "radiantly and romantically symbolic of the rise of the proletariat." And in a recent highly sympathetic study of Anderson, which could have been based on historical perspective, Maxwell Geismar has conspicuously glossed over the novel's totalitarian bias. Such misreadings can be traced less to the inadequate sensibilities of these critics than to their wish to preserve an image of Anderson, justified in other contexts, as a deeply plebeian and democratic writer.

Though the portrait of McGregor uncritically anticipates the power-worship, the irrationality, and the asexual fanaticism of modern totalitarian leaders, it would be absurd and melodramatic to conclude that Anderson was a fascist or forerunner of fascism at the time he wrote the novel. All of his political and moral inclinations were always to be quite in the other direction, and he himself was to look back with a blend of dread and awe to *Marching Men*. The theme of the novel was never again to appear in any of his writings, and *Poor White*, to cite but one example, was to be characterized by a precisely opposite attitude to power and to human beings. What then is the source of the painful ideas in *Marching Men*? One may point to literary influences—Carlyle, mentioned favorably in an article Anderson wrote in the early 1900's, and Jack London, whose Nietzschean notions were then floating through the American intellectual atmosphere— but surely these could hardly account for so thorough a defense of political mindlessness as *Marching Men*.

In part, the novel can be related to Anderson's personal situation. If *Windy McPherson's Son* represents his struggle to make a choice of values in the world of American business, *Marching Men* releases his resentment at the need to think through to that choice. Where *Windy*, because of its intellectual confusion, is limp and diffuse in feeling, *Marching Men* is full of spastic aggression and sadism which reflect undifferentiated anger at the burdens imposed by modern life. And where the earlier novel portrays sexual indecision, the later one conveys a scorn of women and celebrates the brotherhood of a potentially homosexual band. All of these signs of personal crisis were to come to a climax several years later in Anderson's breakdown in 1912.

Yet one feels a need to relate the novel to something more than Anderson's immediate situation, to account for its politics in terms of political influences. Here one can only speculate, and the beginning of such speculation must be the assumption that the ideas of the novel are re-

lated to the intellectual currents of those years in the
late 19th century when Anderson reached his manhood.
Is it then too shocking a violation of the American democratic myth to suggest that some of the emotional qualities, if not the explicit program, oᶜ Anderson's marching
men may be traced back to Populism? That the great-
man theory finds favor only among the upper classes is a
misconception recent history has quite dispelled: the
wealthy scorn a parvenu messiah, except perhaps during
moments of extreme social crisis. Actually, the search for a
leader who through the exertion of his will can lead the
helpless and confused out of the wilderness is distinctly
though not exclusively plebeian, very often related to a
lower-middle-class desire, which is shared by declassed
elements, for a violently dynamic alternative to radicalism. And in *Marching Men* Anderson contemptuously refers to socialists as people who merely wag their jaws,
which is precisely the way a modern totalitarian speaks
of those of his opponents who profess to base their views
on reason.

It is commonly believed that the Populist movement
was a righteous democratic uprising of the people against
the trusts and railroads—which, in part, it certainly was.
But in Populism there was also an insistently program-
matic mindlessness, a mindlessness that was sometimes its
only program; a xenophobic scorn of city slickers and intellectual "long-hairs" who "jawed" about ideas when
immediate action was needed; an occasional stereotyped
identification of the Jew with the odious Wall Street
banker; a sentimental glorification of mere solidarity at the
expense of thought; and a prostrating infatuation with
the eloquent leader whose voice cried out against crosses

of gold and spoke for the inarticulate surge in the hearts of his followers. With the exception of the occasional anti-Semitism, all of these traits are present in *Marching Men*, though they are placed in an urban setting and presented with a crude harshness no Populist could accept. To suggest that Anderson's novel provides a historically faithful portrait of Populism would be merely malicious, but it does not seem malicious to say that it reveals an ignored aspect of that movement. The blend of leader-worship and impatience with ideas present in *Marching Men* is also to be found in the undersides of Populism; it comprises an authoritarian tendency buried deep within a certain kind of plebeian revolt.

As a novel, even for a study of Anderson's apprenticeship, *Marching Men* is of slight interest, but as an expression of ideas it remains highly relevant. It represents the price Anderson was to pay, and which he never quite reckoned, for his failure to assume the responsibilities of the mind; a price he would pay again and again.

Mid-American Chants, Anderson's third book, is a small volume of free verse written after his arrival in Chicago in 1913. The book, which sold only 200 copies, seems to have convinced John Lane that Anderson had no literary future, and led to the firm's rejection of his next book as too gloomy. The next book was *Winesburg, Ohio*.

"Some day, when the spirit moves me," Harry Hansen quotes Anderson as saying, "I am going to that piano and play for you, and I won't need a knowledge of the piano to express myself. I will play what is in me." Anderson's verse was written on much the same principle, and as invariably happens the artist who does not know his instrument is unable to "play what is in me." Aside from an occasional phrase or a rare rhythmic turn, the *Chants* are quite fuzzy in language and feeling. They are self-indulgent calls to poetry affecting the Whitman-Sandburg manner, perhaps even samples of verbal materials close to poetry; but they are not poems.

The *Chants* mirror Anderson's preoccupations at the time he began his best work. Their dominant theme is a sense of dismay at the formlessness of American life and a wish to establish some means to communion ("Out of the mud at the river's edge I molded myself a god, /A grotesque little god with a twisted face,/ A god for myself and my man.") In almost all of the chants the symbol of health is corn, which for Anderson suggests both the vital life destroyed by industrialism and the principle of phallic power. Far more than their rather ceremonial allegiance to the Midwest, the chants reflect Anderson's wish to assert his male certainty ("the milk of the corn is in me") and thereby his bardic leadership of the people ("In the cornfields the sacred vessel is set up. I will renew in my people the worship of gods"). In his later and more valuable work these themes will reappear.

Of his early writing Anderson was to say that it was marred by the excessive influence of other writers, but this is a rather questionable judgment. *Windy McPherson's Son* has often been found derivative from *The Financier*, but Anderson's novel was written before Dreiser's was published. The only book by Dreiser that could have influenced Anderson's first two novels is *Sister Carrie*, and in view of its limited circulation Anderson's claim that he had not read it until after reaching Chicago is probably true. Nor is there any internal evidence that *Sister Carrie* shaped the style or subject matter of Anderson's first two novels. The only influences that may conceivably be detected in *Windy McPherson's Son* and *Marching Men* are the early social novels of H. G. Wells and the radical-adventure stories of Jack London. The truth is that Anderson's early novels were all too much his own, reflecting in their style the natural inclination of a poorly educated writer to strain for the literary and lapse into the colloquial. But if the clumsiness and amateurishness are Anderson's own, so are the occasional passages of talent; passages that point to the possibility of an achievement only later to be realized.

The Book of the Grotesque

BETWEEN Sherwood Anderson's apprentice novels and *Winesburg, Ohio* there stands no intermediary work indicating a gradual growth of talent. *Mid-American Chants* testifies to both an increasing interest in the possibilities of language and a conscious submission to literary influence, but it is hardly a qualitative advance over its predecessors. From Anderson's Elyria work to the achievement that is *Winesburg* there is so abrupt a creative ascent that one wonders what elements in his Chicago experience, whether in reading or personal relations, might have served to release his talents.

The list of writers to whom Anderson acknowledged a serious debt was small: George Borrow, Mark Twain, Ivan Turgeniev. In the early 1920's D. H. Lawrence was added to the small group of masters who had decisively impinged on him, but in 1915 and 1916, the years when he wrote *Winesburg,* Anderson had, of course, not yet read Lawrence.

While his attachment to Borrow antedates his public career as a writer, it also testifies to a wish, once that career had begun, to fondle a certain image of himself as a literary personality. To Anderson, the artist always seemed a peculiarly fortunate being who could evade much of the drabness of daily life. By ordering his experience through the canny artifice available only to himself, the artist could establish a margin for the half-forgotten life of flair and largesse, could find a way of surmounting the barren passage of the routine. Unlike those American writers who take great pains to insist that their occupation is as "normal" as any other, Anderson liked to proclaim the uniqueness of the artist's life.

To a writer enamored of such a notion, the figure of George Borrow would naturally seem attractive. Borrow's picturesque narratives of gypsy life, virtually unclassifiable among the traditional genres, seemed significant to Anderson because they flowed from a conscious rejection of conventionality and charming because they did not flinch from the romantic, the garrulous, and the merely odd. Borrow provided Anderson with an image of a potential self: the sympathetic auditor of his people's inner history; and for the Borrovian hero who wanders among "backward peoples" he had a considerable admiration, particularly during those burdened years in Elyria when he thought the literary career an avenue to a liberated and adventurous life. Yet there are no significant traces of Borrow in any of Anderson's books; neither in subject matter nor in structure is there an observable line of descent from, say, *Lavengro* to *Winesburg*. The relation is one of personal identification rather than literary influence; Borrow, it seemed to Anderson, was above all a guide to how a writer might live.

If Borrow suggested an attractive style of life, Turgeniev's *Memoirs of a Sportsman,* "like low fine music," set the very tone Anderson wished to strike in his prose. In Turgeniev's masterpiece he admired most that purity of feeling which comes from creative tact, from the author's strict refusal to violate or impose himself on his characters. Between *Memoirs of a Sportsman,* which Anderson called "the sweetest thing in all literature," and *Winesburg* there are obvious similarities: both are episodic novels containing loosely bound but closely related sketches, both depend for impact less on dramatic action than on a climactic lyrical insight, and in both the individual sketches frequently end with bland understatements that form an ironic coda to the body of the writing. These similarities could certainly be taken as tokens of influence—if only we were certain that Anderson had actually read Turgeniev before writing *Winesburg.*

When critics in the 1920's discovered that Anderson was indebted to Chekhov and Dostoievsky (which he was not), he gleefully denied having known the Russian novelists until after the publication of *Winesburg.* This denial, however, is controverted by two statements in his correspondence, a remark in his *Memoirs,* and a recollection in an autobiographical fragment. His credibility as a witness of his own past is further damaged by the fact that in the early 1920's his publisher, probably at his instigation and certainly with his consent, issued a public statement denying that Anderson had read *Spoon River* before writing *Winesburg* and insisting that Masters's book appeared after the *Winesburg* sketches came out in magazines. Though the publisher was wrong on both counts, Anderson did not trouble to correct him. Like many untrained writers, he may have feared that an acknowledgment of a literary debt would cast doubt on the value or at least the originality of his work.

But if Turgeniev's influence on *Winesburg* is not quite certain, there can be no doubt about Mark Twain's. Between the America of Anderson's boyhood, which is the setting of his best work, and the America of Huck Finn there are only a few intervening decades, and the nostalgia for a lost moment of American pastoral which saturates *Huckleberry Finn* is also present in *Winesburg*. Twain's influence on Anderson is most obvious in the early portions of *Poor White* and some of the stories in *The Triumph of the Egg*, but it can also be seen in *Winesburg*, particularly in Anderson's attempt to use American speech as the base of a tensed rhythmic style. His identification with Borrow was to some extent a romantic whimsy, but his identification with Twain had a strong basis in reality. As he wrote to Van Wyck Brooks, Twain had also been an untrained man of natural talent "caught up by the dreadful cheap smartness, the shrillness that was a part of the life of the country"; Twain had also been bedeviled by the problem of success and the need to conciliate the pressures of East and West.

These were pervasive influences; none of them could have provided the immediate shock, the specific impetus that turned Anderson to the style and matter of *Winesburg*. Such an impetus, if one can be singled out at all, came not from any individual writer but from Anderson's dramatic exposure in 1913-15 to the Chicago literary world. When Max Wald, one of "the little children of the arts," lent him a copy of *Spoon River*, Anderson raced through it in a night. This, he excitedly told his friends, is the real thing—by which he meant that Masters, in his imaginary Midwestern village, had bared the hidden lesions of the American psyche. Had Anderson stopped to notice the appalling frustration that motivated Masters's book he might have been somewhat less enthusiastic, but for the moment *Spoon River* suggested that in a prose equivalent Anderson might find a form allowing more freedom than the conventional novel and yet resulting in greater complexity of meaning than could be had in any individual sketch. Masters hardly influenced the vision behind *Winesburg*, but he did provide intimations of how it might be organized.

At about the same time Anderson was introduced by his brother Karl to the early writings of Gertrude Stein. Anderson has recalled that he "had come to Gertrude Stein's book about which everyone laughed but about which I did not laugh. It excited me as one might grow excited in going into a new and wonderful country where everything is strange. . . ." The truth, however, was somewhat more complex than Anderson's memory. His first reactions to Stein were antagonistic: at a Chicago party in 1915 he told Edna Kenton that he thought it merely funny that anyone should take *Tender Buttons* seriously, and shortly afterwards he even composed a parody of Stein for his advertising cronies.

But his inaccurate recollection had, as usual, a point of genuine relevance. For though he laughed at Stein when he first read her, she seems to have stimulated him in a way few other writers could. Nearly always one parodies, for good or bad, those writers who deeply matter. To Anderson, Stein suggested that, at least in the actual process of composition, words could have an independent value:

they could be fresh or stale, firm or gruelly, colored or drab. After reading the fanatically monosyllabic *Three Lives* Anderson would hardly try again, as he had in his first two novels, to write "literary" English. But despite such surface similarities as repetition of key words and an insistently simple syntax, their styles had little in common. Stein's language was opaque, leading back into itself and thereby tending to replace the matter of fiction, while the language of *Winesburg* was translucent, leading quickly to the center of the book's action. Stein was the best kind of influence: she did not bend Anderson to her style, she liberated him for his own.

And that, essentially, was what the Chicago literary milieu did. It persuaded Anderson that American writers needed an indigenous style which, if only they were bold enough, they could then and there construct; it taught him that before language could be used creatively it might have to be crumbled into particles; and it made him conscious of the need for literary consciousness. For the time being that was enough.

Anderson has recalled that during the years immediately preceding *Winesburg* he would often take with him on advertising trips pages torn from Gideon Bibles, which he read over and over again. This recollection tells us most of what needs to be known about the making of *Winesburg*. Its author had not the slightest interest in religion, but his first involvement in a literary environment had made him aware of writing as writing and had taught him where to find its greatest English source. He had begun to work as a conscious craftsman: the resulting ferment was *Mid-American Chants*, the substance *Winesburg*.

The history of *Winesburg* is a curious instance of the way criticism, with its passion for "placing," can reduce a writer to harmless irrelevance. At various times the book has been banished to such categories as the revolt against the village, the rejection of middle-class morality, the proclamation of sexual freedom, and the rise of cultural primitivism. Whatever the justification for such tags may once have been, it is now quite obvious that Anderson's revolt was directed against something far more fundamental than the restrictions of the American village and was, for that matter, equally relevant to the American city; that *Winesburg* is not primarily concerned with morality, middle-class or otherwise, if only because most of its characters are not in a position to engage in moral choice; that while its subject is frequently tangential to sex it expresses no opinions about and offers no proposals for sexual conduct, free or restricted; and that its style is only dimly related to anything that might be called primitive. If read as social fiction *Winesburg* is somewhat absurd, for no such town could possibly exist. If read as a venture into abnormal psychology the book seems almost lurid, for within its total structure the behavior of its hysterics and paranoids is quite purposeless and, in the absence of any norms to which their deviations might be compared, even incomprehensible. In fact, if read according to the usual expectations of 20th-century naturalistic or conventionally realistic fiction, *Winesburg* seems incoherent and the charge of emotion it can still raise inexplicable.

In its fundamental quality *Winesburg* is nonrealistic; it does not seek to gratify the eye with a verisimilitude to social forms in the way a Dreiser or a Lewis novel does.

In rather shy lyrical outbursts the book conveys a vision of American life as a depressed landscape cluttered with dead stumps, twisted oddities, grotesque and pitiful wrecks; a landscape in which ghosts fumble erratically and romance is reduced to mere fugitive brushings at night; a landscape eerie with the cracked echoes of village queers rambling in their lonely eccentricity. Again and again *Winesburg* suggests that beneath the exteriors of our life the deformed exert dominion, that the seeming health of our state derives from a deep malignancy. And *Winesburg* echoes with American loneliness, that loneliness which could once evoke Nigger Jim's chant of praise to the Mississippi pastoral but which has here become fearful and sour.

Winesburg is a book largely set in twilight and darkness, its backgrounds heavily shaded with gloomy blacks and marshy grays—as is proper for a world of withered men who, sheltered by night, reach out for that sentient life they dimly recall as the racial inheritance that has been squandered away. Like most fiction, *Winesburg* is a variation on the theme of reality and appearance, in which the deformations caused by day (public life) are intensified at night and, in their very extremity, become an entry to reality. From Anderson's instinctively right placement of the book's central actions at twilight and night comes some of its frequently noticed aura of "lostness"—as if the most sustaining and fruitful human activities can no longer be performed in public communion but must be grasped in secret.

The two dozen central figures in *Winesburg* are hardly characters in the usual novelistic sense. They are not shown in depth or breadth, complexity or ambiguity;

they are allowed no variations of action or opinion; they do not, with the exception of George Willard, the book's "hero," grow or decline. For Anderson is not trying to represent through sensuous images the immediate surface of human experience; he is rather drawing the abstract and deliberately distorted paradigm of an extreme situation, and for that purpose fully rounded characterizations could only be a complicating blemish.

The figures of *Winesburg* usually personify to fantastic excess a condition of psychic deformity which is the consequence of some crucial failure in their lives, some aborted effort to extend their personalities or proffer their love. Misogyny, inarticulateness, frigidity, God-infatuation, homosexuality, drunkenness—these are symptoms of their recoil from the regularities of human intercourse and sometimes of their substitute gratifications in inanimate objects, as with the unloved Alice Hindman who "because it was her own, could not bear to have anyone touch the furniture of her room." In their compulsive traits these figures find a kind of dulling peace, but as a consequence they are subject to rigid monomanias and are deprived of one of the great blessings of human health: the capacity for a variety of experience. That is why, in a sense, "nothing happens" in *Winesburg*. For most of its figures it is too late for anything to happen, they can only muse over the traumas which have so harshly limited their spontaneity. Stripped of their animate wholeness and twisted into frozen postures of defense, they are indeed what Anderson has called them: grotesques.

The world of *Winesburg*, populated largely by these back-street grotesques, soon begins to seem like a buried ruin of a once vigorous society, an atrophied remnant of the egalitarian moment of 19th-century America. Though many of the book's sketches are placed in the out-of-doors, its atmosphere is as stifling as a tomb. And the reiteration of the term "grotesque" is felicitous in a way Anderson could hardly have been aware of; for it was first used by Renaissance artists to describe arabesques painted in the underground ruins, *grotte*, of Nero's "Golden House."

The conception of the grotesque, as actually developed in the stories, is not merely that it is an unwilled affliction but also that it is a mark of a once sentient striving. In his introductory fantasy, "The Book of the Grotesque," Anderson writes: "It was the truths that made the people grotesques . . . the moment one of the people took one of the truths to himself, called it his truth, and tried to live his life by it, he became a grotesque and the truth he embraced a falsehood." There is a sense, as will be seen later, in which these sentences are at variance with the book's meaning, but they do suggest the significant notion that the grotesques are those who *have* sought "the truths" that disfigure them. By contrast the banal creatures who dominate the town's official life, such as Will Henderson, publisher of the paper for which George Willard works, are not even grotesques: they are simply clods. The grotesques are those whose humanity has been outraged and who, to survive in Winesburg, have had to suppress their wish to love. Wash Williams becomes a misogynist because his mother-in-law, hoping to reconcile him to his faithless wife, thrusts her into his presence naked; Wing Biddlebaum becomes a recluse because his wish to blend learning with affection is fatally misunderstood. Grotesqueness, then, is not merely the shield of deformity; it is also a remnant of misshapen feeling, what Dr. Reefy in "Paper Pills" calls "the sweetness of the twisted apples."

Winesburg may thus be read as a fable of American estrangement, its theme the loss of love. The book's major characters are alienated from the basic sources of emotional sustenance—from the nature in which they live but to which they can no longer have an active relationship; from the fertility of the farms that flank them but no longer fulfill their need for creativity; from the community which, at least by the claim of the American mythos, once bound men together in fraternity but is now merely an institution external to their lives; from the work which once evoked and fulfilled their sense of craft but is now a mere burden; and, most catastrophic of all, from each other, the very extremity of their need for love having itself become a barrier to its realization.

The grotesques rot because they are unused, their energies deprived of outlet, and their instincts curdled in isolation. As Waldo Frank has noticed in his fine study of *Winesburg*, the first three stories in the book suggest this view in a complete theme-statement. The story, "Hands," through several symbolic referents, depicts the loss of creativity in the use of the human body. The second story, "Paper Pills," directly pictures the progressive ineffectuality of human thought, pocketed in paper pellets that no one reads. And the third story, "Mother," relates these two themes to a larger variant: the inability of Elizabeth Willard, *Winesburg's* mother-figure, to communicate her love to her son. "The form of the mother, frustrate, lonely, at last desperate," Frank writes, "pervades the variations that make the rest of the book: a continuity of variation swelling, swirling into the corners and crannies of the village life; and at last closing in the mother's death, in the loss forever of the $800 which Elizabeth Willard had kept for twenty years to give her son his start away from Winesburg, and in the son's wistful departure." In the rupture of family love and the consequent loss of George Willard's heritage, the theme-statement of the book is completed.

The book's central strand of action, discernible in about half the stories, is the effort of the grotesques to establish intimate relations with George Willard, the young reporter. At night, when they need not fear the mockery of public detection, they hesitantly approach him, almost in supplication, to tell him of their afflictions and perhaps find health in his voice. Instinctively, they sense his moral freshness, finding hope in the fact that he has not yet been calloused by knowledge and time. To some of the grotesques, such as Dr. Reefy and Dr. Parcival, George Willard is the lost son returned, the Daedalus whose apparent innocence and capacity for feeling will redeem Winesburg. To others among the grotesques, such as Tom Foster and Elmer Cowley, he is a reporter-messenger, a small-town Hermes, bringing news of a dispensation which will allow them to re-enter the world of men. But perhaps most fundamentally and subsuming these two visions, he seems to the grotesques a young priest who will renew the forgotten communal rites by which they may again be bound together. To Louise Trunnion he will bring a love that is more than a filching of flesh; to Dr. Parcival the promise to "write the book that I may never get written" in which he will tell all men that "everyone in the world is Christ and they are all crucified"; to the Reverend Curtis Hartman the willingness to understand a vision of God as revealed in the flesh of a naked woman; to Wash Williams the peace that will ease his sense of violation; and to Enoch Robinson the "youthful sadness, young man's sadness, the sadness of a growing boy in a village at the year's end [which can open] the lips of the old man."

As they approach George Willard, the grotesques seek not merely the individual release of a sudden expressive outburst, but also a relation with each other that may restore them to collective harmony. They are distraught communicants in search of a ceremony, a social value, a manner of living, a lost ritual that may, by some means, re-establish a flow and exchange of emotion. Their estrangement is so extreme that they cannot turn to each other though it is each other they really need and secretly want; they turn instead to George Willard who will soon be out of the orbit of their life. The miracle that the Reverend Curtis Hartman sees and the message over which Kate Swift broods could bind one to the other, yet they both turn to George Willard who, receptive though he may wish to be, cannot understand them.

In only one story, "Death," do the grotesques seem to meet. Elizabeth Willard and Dr. Reefy embrace in a moment of confession, but their approach to love is interrupted by a stray noise. Elizabeth leaves: "The thing that had come to life in her as she talked to her one friend died suddenly." A few months later, at her deathbed, Dr. Reefy meets George Willard and puts out "his hand as though to greet the young man and then awkwardly [draws] it back again." Bloom does not find his Daedalus;

the hoped-for epiphany comes at the verge of death and, as in all the stories, is aborted; the ritual of communal love remains unrealized.

The burden which the grotesques would impose on George Willard is beyond his strength. He is not yet himself a grotesque mainly because he has not yet experienced very deeply, but for the role to which they would assign him he is too absorbed in his own ambition and restlessness. The grotesques see in his difference from them the possibility of saving themselves, but actually it is the barrier to an ultimate companionship. George Willard's adolescent receptivity to the grotesques can only give him the momentary emotional illumination described in that lovely story, "Sophistication." On the eve of his departure from Winesburg, George Willard reaches the point "when he for the first time takes the backward view of life. . . . With a little gasp he sees himself as merely a leaf blown by the wind through the streets of his village. He knows that in spite of all the stout talk of his fellows he must live and die in uncertainty, a thing blown by the winds, a thing destined like corn to wilt in the sun. . . . Already he hears death calling. With all his heart he wants to come close to some other human, touch someone with all his hands. . . ." For George this illumination is enough, but it is not for the grotesques. They are a moment in his education, he a confirmation of their doom. "I have missed something. I have missed something Kate Swift was trying to tell me," he says to himself one night as he falls asleep. He has missed the meaning of Kate Swift's life: it is not his fault: her salvation, like the salvation of the other grotesques, is beyond his capacities.

In the story "Queer" these meanings receive their most

generalized expression, for its grotesque, Elmer Cowley,
has no specific deformity: he is the grotesque as such. "He
was, he felt, one condemned to go through life without
friends and he hated the thought." Wishing to talk to
George Willard, he loses courage and instead rants to a
half-wit: "I had to tell some one and you were the only
one I could tell. I hunted out another queer one, you see.
I ran away, that's what I did." When Elmer Cowley
does call George Willard out of the newspaper office, he
again becomes tongue-tied in his presence. Despairing
over "his failure to declare his determination not to be
queer," Elmer Cowley decides to leave Winesburg, but in
a last effort at communication he asks George Willard to
meet him at the midnight local. Again he cannot speak.
"Elmer Cowley danced with fury beside the groaning
train in the darkness on the station platform. . . . Like
one struggling for release from hands that held him he
struck, hitting George Willard blow after blow on the
breast, the neck, the mouth." Unable to give Elmer
Cowley the love that might dissolve his queerness, George
Willard suffers the fate of the rejected priest.

From the story "Queer," it is possible to abstract the
choreography of *Winesburg*. Its typical action is a series
of dance maneuvers by figures whose sole distinctive characteristic is an extreme deformity of movement or posture. Each of these grotesques dances, with angular indirection and muted pathos, toward a central figure who
seems to them young, fresh, and radiant. For a moment
they seem to draw close to him and thereby to abandon
their stoops and limps, but this moment quickly dissolves
in the play of the dance and perhaps it never even existed: the central figure cannot be reached. Slowly and

painfully, the grotesques withdraw while the young man leaves the stage entirely. None of the grotesques is seen full-face for more than a moment, and none of them is individually important to the scheme of the dance. For this is a dance primarily of spatial relationships rather than solo virtuosity; the distances established between the dancers, rather than their personalities, form the essence of the dance. And in the end, its meaning is revealed in the fact that all but the one untouched youth return to precisely their original places and postures.

When Anderson first sent his *Winesburg* stories to the *Masses, Seven Arts,* and the *Little Review,* he intended each of them to be a self-contained unit, as in fact they may still be regarded. But there was clearly a unifying conception behind all the stories: they were set in the same locale, many of the characters appeared in several stories, and there was a remarkable consistency of mood that carried over from story to story. Consequently, when Anderson prepared them for book publication in 1919, he had only to make a few minor changes, mostly insertions of place and character names as connectives, in order to have a unified book.

Particularly if approached along the lines that have been suggested here, *Winesburg* seems remarkably of a piece. The only stories that do not fit into its pattern are the four-part narrative of Jesse Bentley, a failure in any case, and possibly "The Untold Lie," a beautiful story measuring the distance between middle-age and youth. Of the others only "Tandy" is so bad that its omission would help the book. On the other hand, few of the stories read as well in isolation as in the book's context.

Except for "Hands," "The Strength of God," "Paper Pills," and "The Untold Lie," they individually lack the dramatic power which the book has as a whole.

Winesburg is an excellently formed piece of fiction, each of its stories following a parabola of movement which abstractly graphs the book's meaning. From a state of feeling rather than a dramatic conflict there develops in one of the grotesques a rising lyrical excitement, usually stimulated to intensity by the presence of George Willard. At the moment before reaching a climax, this excitement is frustrated by a fatal inability at communication and then it rapidly dissolves into its original diffuse base. This structural pattern is sometimes varied by an ironic turn, as in "Nobody Knows" and "A Man of Ideas," but in only one story, "Sophistication," is the emotional ascent allowed to move forward without interruption.

But the unity of the book depends on more than the congruous design of its parts. The first three stories of *Winesburg* develop its major theme, which, after several variations, reaches its most abstract version in "Queer." The stories following "Queer" seem somewhat of a thematic afterthought, though they are necessary for a full disposal of the characters. The one conspicuous disharmony in the book is that the introductory "Book of the Grotesque" suggests that the grotesques are victims of their wilful fanaticism, while in the stories themselves grotesqueness is the result of an essentially valid resistance to forces external to its victims.

Through a few simple but extremely effective symbols, the stories are both related to the book's larger meaning and defined in their uniqueness. For the former of these purposes, the most important symbol is that of the room, frequently used to suggest isolation and confinement. Kate Swift is alone in her bedroom, Dr. Reefy in his office, the Reverend Curtis Hartman in his church tower, Enoch Robinson in his fantasy-crowded room. Enoch Robinson's story "is in fact the story of a room almost more than it is the story of a man." The tactful use of this symbol lends *Winesburg* a claustrophobic aura appropriate to its theme.

Most of the stories are further defined by symbols related to their particular meanings. The story of the misogynist Wash Williams begins by rapidly thrusting before the reader an image of "a huge, grotesque kind of monkey, a creature with ugly sagging, hairless skin," which dominates its subsequent action. And more valid than any abstract statement of theme is the symbolic power of that moment in "The Strength of God" when the Reverend Curtis Hartman, in order to peek into Kate Swift's bedroom, breaks his church window at precisely the place where the figure of a boy stands "motionless and looking with rapt eyes into the face of Christ."

Though *Winesburg* is written in the bland accents of the American story teller, it has an economy impossible to oral narration because Anderson varies the beat of its accents by occasionally whipping them into quite formal rhetorical patterns. In the book's best stretches there is a tension between its underlying loose oral cadences and the stiffened superimposed beat of a prose almost Biblical in its regularity. Anderson's prose is neither "natural" nor primitive; it is rather a hushed bardic chant, low-toned and elegiacally awkward, deeply related to native speech rhythms yet very much the result of literary cultivation.

But the final effectiveness of this prose is in its prevalent tone of tender inclusiveness. Between writer and materials there is an admirable equity of relationship. None of the characters is violated, none of the stories, even the failures, leaves the reader with the bitter sense of having been tricked by cleverness or cheapness or toughness. The ultimate unity of the book is a unity of feeling, a sureness of warmth, and a readiness to accept Winesburg's lost grotesques with the embrace of humility. Many American writers have taken as their theme the loss of love in the modern world, but few, if any at all, have so thoroughly realized it in the accents of love.

Conditions of Fame

IN THE last years of his life, when Anderson looked back to the history of his most famous book, he wrote that *Winesburg* was "widely condemned, called nasty and dirty. . . . In review after review it was called 'a sewer' and the man who had written it taken as a strangely sex-obsessed man. . . . Every now and then a man declares that, when the book was first published he praised it, but if there was any such praise, at the time, it escaped my notice." Anderson was particularly vehement in denying H. L. Mencken's claim to have recognized immediately the book's merit.

This recollection seems a mere fantasy, for actually *Winesburg* received highly favorable reviews. *The New Republic* said that "nothing better has come out of America," *The Liberator* called the book "a magnificent collection of tales," and Hart Crane wrote that "America should read this book on her knees. It constitutes an important chapter in the Bible of her consciousness." But even if such reviews did "escape" Anderson's notice, it is inconceivable that he failed to see the favorable comments in the Chicago press, particularly H. L. Mencken's praise of *Winesburg* as "very remarkable." There were a few attacks, such as the sneer of the conservative *New York Sun* that the book was "A Gutter [that] Would Be Spoon River," but by and large it was received as an important work of American fiction. As Anderson himself wrote to Waldo Frank shortly after it appeared: "I get constant and beautiful reactions from [sic] *Winesburg*."

Why then were these "beautiful reactions" remembered twenty years later as "nasty and dirty"? Part of the answer may be that in the late 1930's, when Anderson was suffering from painfully harsh criticism, he was led into distorting the history of *Winesburg's* reception by the attacks on *Beyond Desire* and *Kit Brandon*. To have acknowledged that *Winesburg* was praised on its appearance would have meant abandoning the wistful notion that the later books were being disparaged because they were bold and unconventional. And it is also possible that his seeming paramnesia about *Winesburg's* critical history was related to his complaint that, at the hands of Ben Huebsch, his new publisher, "it was more than two years selling its first five thousand"—a quite good sale, as it happens, for a book of serious short stories.

But these explanations do not seem sufficient, and it must therefore be surmised that Anderson's complaint about the reviews of *Winesburg* was partly an echo of the insecurity he had felt during the years when the book was written. In those years he had begun to sense the limitations of the Chicago milieu and to establish eager relations with New York literary people, but since the New York intellectuals seemed to him far more accomplished than those in Chicago, his feeling of inferiority toward intellectuals as a group was still further aggravated. In 1916 Anderson had begun corresponding with a young New York writer, Waldo Frank, who had asked him to contribute to *The Seven Arts*, a new magazine Frank was to edit with Van Wyck Brooks and James Oppenheim. Anderson had sent Frank his excellent story, "The Untold Lie," which had so excited Frank that he wrote an article on Anderson, "Emerging Greatness," for the magazine's first issue. It was consequently an important moment for Anderson when he visited the *Seven Arts* office in the winter of 1917. At first his appearance left the editors somewhat nonplussed, for, as Oppenheim was to recall, "I had built an Anderson out of the stories, a shy sort of fellow, a little mussed, slipping against the wall so as not to occupy too much space. Instead of that I looked straight at an up-and-coming ad man with a stiff collar, and a bit of the super-salesman air." But once they accepted the fact that Anderson neither looked nor had to look like a Winesburg grotesque, the *Seven Arts* editors thought him all the more a miracle.

Anderson and Frank quickly became intimate friends, exchanging in their letters compliments and opinions that, for a while, each found richly sustaining. In the summer of 1917 Anderson persuaded Frank to come to Lake Chateaugay where he and Tennessee were vacationing. The following summer Frank accompanied Anderson to Wisconsin for a vacation. And in the summer of 1919 Frank visited Anderson in Chicago where, at the latter's insistence, they bought creamy white pongee suits which proved a sensation among their friends. To the self-conscious Frank this too seemed part of his necessary immersion in American experience.

Though Frank was to be his most intimate literary friend until about 1922, Anderson also established close relations with Van Wyck Brooks and Paul Rosenfeld, both of whom were gaining reputations as liberating young critics. If to these names is added that of Hart Crane, with whom Anderson began corresponding in 1919, the list of his close literary friends during these years is complete. By praising the young poet's work and writing to him about his own experience as a businessman, Anderson gave Crane a sense of hope and perspective; Crane, as yet, could give him little in return. For the sustenance he needed, Anderson turned to Frank, Brooks, and Rosenfeld, who seemed to him the very paragons of cosmopolitan culture.

In its prospectus *The Seven Arts* had declared that America had reached "that national self-consciousness which is the beginning of greatness." It can easily be maintained that this statement means nothing at all, but at the moment it did signify that Frank and, to a lesser extent, Brooks were sated with the traditional culture in which they had been educated and now intended to search for the indigenous, the unspoiled, and the anti-Puritanical. In Anderson Frank saw the native genius at its sweetest, the uncontaminated voice rising from the middle plains; and because he needed the native and un-contaminated Frank fell in love with Anderson's gift, his personality, his color—most of all, with the idea of Anderson. "To me, the young New Yorker," Frank has recalled, "Sherwood Anderson was America; the discovery of him was an exhilarating part of my discovery of my own country. And to him, his New York friends . . . represented *le grand monde* of intellect and culture." Brooks has similarly written that "While most of us were Easterners, we felt that the heart of America lay in the West; and Sherwood was the essence of his West."

Frank, a more passionate and effusive man than Brooks, sent Anderson long letters in which he declared his vision of a culture free from the Puritan clamp and a nation "whole" rather than fragmented. Anderson, in turn, wrote of his struggle for literary articulation and his deep identification with mid-America. Sometimes they seem to have been interested in each other less as human beings than as symbols of their needs, Frank's need for integration and Anderson's for enrichment; sometimes one suspects in their letters a thin strand of guile, Frank's guile arising from a wilful insistence that Anderson be *the* American artist and Anderson's from a self-conscious readiness to adapt himself to Frank's image. But such strictures should not be taken as a denial of the real and moving camaraderie they established; and if it now seems a bit excessive for them to have opened their letters with "Dear Brother" and to have closed them with "Love," that impression may well be due to a later generation's incapacity for a willed affirmation. Even for a reticent literary generation it is not too difficult to understand why Frank should have heard an authentic American voice in certain passages of Anderson's letters:

> Is it not likely that when the country was new and men were often alone in the fields and the forest they got a sense of bigness outside themselves that has now in some way been lost. . . . Mystery whispered in the grass, played in the branches of trees overhead, was caught up and blown across the American line in clouds of dust at evening on the prairies.
>
> I am old enough to remember tales that strengthen my belief in a deep semi-religious influence that was

formerly at work among our people. The flavor of it hangs over the best work of Mark Twain. . . . I can remember old fellows in my home town speaking feelingly of an evening spent on the big empty plains. It had taken the shrillness out of them. They had learned the trick of quiet. . . .

And when Anderson, in a more personal vein, wrote,

I care not a damn what you are thinking. . . . What I do care is how are you brother? How blows the wind, how falls the morning light on the bed where you sleep?

Frank could feel that here at last was the creative comradeship for which he had yearned. What he gave Anderson in return was a sense of how lofty the artist's dedication could be; a sense that the life of art meant, not necessarily the personal release with which Anderson had always associated it, but the possibility of a creative satisfaction no other kind of life could yield. Frank encouraged Anderson to trust himself, his own instincts and voices—and sometimes Anderson trusted himself a bit too much, as when he took up painting during a 1920 vacation in Alabama and with egregious naïveté wrote to Frank, "By disregarding all roads taken by other painters I have seen, I have already found out some things."

The friendship between Anderson and Brooks was rather more austere, though as important for Anderson's development as a writer. In Brooks, Anderson felt he had found a guide to the American past at least as competent as Frank to the European present, and through Brooks he learned to identify himself with the plebeian literary tradition that had its sources in Lincoln, Whitman, and

Twain. Brooks's famous essay, "Highbrows and Low-brows" particularly impressed him. (How revealing that to articulate his sense of kinship with Mark Twain Anderson had to read the criticism of Brooks, an eastern intellectual!) Unfortunately, Anderson did not always appropriate Brooks's views with care or intelligence. Reviewing Brooks's *Letters and Leadership*, he praised Brooks for pointing to a literature "truer, more real and more a part of ourselves than the oversentimental and inanely optimistic literature of our past"—a remark that merely exposed his painful ignorance of 19th-century American writing.

Edmund Wilson has remarked that in Anderson's letters to Brooks "one still hears . . . an echo of the imperfect understanding between Walt Whitman and Emerson." Wilson's observation is true, most conspicuously for Anderson's unsuccessful attempt to convince Brooks that the core of Mark Twain is Huck Finn the boy and *Huckleberry Finn* the book. While Brooks was working on his *Ordeal of Mark Twain* Anderson warned him: "I get in some odd way a sense of the fact that you want constantly to write of men like Twain and Whitman but draw back from their imperfections, their looseness of thought, their vulgarities. . . . Surely the thing has to be undertaken as a labor of love and love should stomach imperfections." Anderson was largely right, as Brooks himself was later to acknowledge, but there is more to his letters than this echo of the imperfect understanding between Whitman and Emerson. There is that imperfect understanding made self-conscious and artful by its deliberate cultivation—artful in the way that only the self-consciously folk writer can sometimes be. In writing to Brooks Anderson could not feel the freedom he felt in writing to Frank; Brooks was not the kind of man who could quickly release the love of his friends; and without love, even the imperfect love he felt for Frank, Anderson soon became too sophisticated in his primitivism, too much the careful novice eager to impress the master.

In no sense whatever was Anderson a trimmer; the help he wanted from Brooks was not for the furthering of his career but for the enrichment of his mind. Anderson clearly saw Brooks's great talent as a critic and literary leader—as two decades later, in referring to Brooks as a general who had deserted his army, he was to see how badly that talent had been misused. But even as he hoped that Brooks might become the cultural mentor he had never had, Anderson sensed that Brooks was a man whose inner life was too thickly hedged for such a role. In a letter to Paul Rosenfeld he wrote that Brooks had "in his make-up the beauty and inner cold fright of the New Englander. That's what makes it so difficult for me to feel warm and close to him as I so often do to you and Waldo, although I respect him sometimes more than any other living man." To have noticed thirty years ago the "inner cold fright" of the man who would write *The Flowering of New England* and yet to have respected his talent, was an act of complex and judicious insight; and it helps to explain why Anderson in his letters to Brooks, though yearning for friendship, would strike out with perceptible gestures of aggression.

But such gestures are visible only in retrospect, and undoubtedly in 1919 or 1920 Anderson's only conscious concern with regard to Brooks was to pierce his reserve in

order to draw from his knowledge. The letters are filled
with shy pleas for help:

> Do try to form the habit of writing me some of your
> thoughts occasionally. It is lonely out here. . . .
> When I talked to Waldo out here I felt in him a
> sense of background I have never had. I wondered if
> he knew the [my?] utter lack of background. It means
> so very much that you know and of course he must
> know also. . . .
> What friendship you give strengthens. It is a thing
> that cuts across the darkness and mist. . . .
> Well if you see things in me give me your friend-
> ship as Waldo has done. Let me see your mind at work
> as often as you can. . . .

Almost as much as their intellect, Anderson envied his
eastern literary friends their economic freedom. Frank
and Rosenfeld had private resources, and Brooks managed to live by his literary work. For Anderson, still turning out advertisements in Chicago, the contrast between
their life and his strengthened the feeling that he was
wasting his best years. In 1918 he established a new and
advantageous arrangement with the Critchfield agency;
he set up a little sub-agency, and though he still had to
share fees and clear accounts with Critchfield, he now had
his own office and work schedule. With this new freedom,
he could take frequent trips to New York. But he was
still dissatisfied, and in 1918 he was writing to Brooks: "I
wish my books would sell for one reason. I want to quit
working for a living and go wander for five years in our
towns." Three years later he wrote to Frank: "I shall have
to get out of business at once—within a month perhaps. I
know nothing of how it can be done. I only know it must
be done." And in 1922 when Anderson finally did stop

listing Chicago as his home he also left the advertising
business; from then to the end of his life he would always
try to earn his living by writing.

Difficult as it was to gain the freedom from job-holding
he envied in his eastern friends, Anderson found it still
more difficult to acquire their cultural security, their feeling that they "belonged" in the literary milieu and were
at ease with its tradition. The muted demands he made
on his New York friends they could not satisfy: Brooks
because he was too much involved with himself,
Rosenfeld because he was too much of an intellectual im-
pressionist, and Frank because he was becoming interested
in a philosophical quest that left mere fiction writing far
behind. It is just possible that these three men together
might have been able to save Anderson from the literary and personal debacles of his next two decades; he
clearly needed guidance and they as clearly were the men
best equipped to give it to him. But the conditions of
American life that impoverished Anderson also impoverished them, if in different ways, and they were no more
to blame for their ultimate inability to help Anderson
than he was to blame for needing their help.

Frank, Brooks, and Rosenfeld showed him the true
goals, certainly the best goals then available, but they
also, unwittingly and with the best possible intentions,
made him painfully aware of how inaccessible those goals
were for him. Stark Young, who became friendly with
Anderson a few years later, has remembered his speaking
of Rosenfeld's "wide culture and style as something he
himself could never hope to achieve, showing at the same
time both that he was never going to try for it and that
he was going on feeling this admiration, envy and de-

light. . . . This complicated, warm feeling of Sherwood's is full of matter. It serves to indicate both the respect, amounting almost to awe, that he felt for what seemed to him education, cultivation, finish, and also the fact . . . that it was in Paul—above everyone else—that he found this quality of culture and style represented."

Anderson's public personality, as it developed in the years immediately after the success of *Winesburg*, was at least partly a response to the intellectual milieu of New York. His natural capacity for affection and warmth remained as genuine as ever, but he also felt the need—as how could he not?—to cultivate those of his talents for public vividness that might better have been left dormant. In a letter to Floyd Dell he wrote: "One thing I've known always, instinctively—that's how to handle people, make them do as I please, be what I wanted them to be. I was in business for a long time and the truth is I was a smooth son of a bitch." Anderson is here exaggerating, he was hardly as smooth as all that; but it is undoubtedly true that his relations with his friends were not quite so spontaneous as they might have been. The Midwestern plebeian made self-conscious could hardly avoid artiness; the writer whose literary creed was the rejection of trickiness found himself crowded into a position where he had to summon the calculating shrewdness of a side-show barker; the artist whose rapport with the natural was a major source of his creativity found himself drifting into the contrived; and the man who wanted, as did perhaps no one else in his time, the released energies of love, felt himself so besieged by pressures that he viewed almost everyone with suspicion and, sometimes, fear. The worst of it was that the self-consciousness was unavoidable: how could he be happy or relaxed when he had to acknowledge men like Frank and Rosenfeld, many years his juniors, as teachers whom in some respects he could never equal? When Anderson went to literary parties, he would always listen with the greatest respect to intellectual talk—until, his admiration overcome by envy, he would break in with one of his marvelously told, slightly off-color anecdotes and draw the center of the party to himself. Had he by some mysterious process of insulation been able to maintain his old life of comparative obscurity or, once famous, to acclimate himself to the intellectuals, Anderson might have come through the post-*Winesburg* period intact; but his tragedy was that neither of these alternatives was possible.

The recollections of two of his closest friends, both of whom always felt strong affection for him, support this view. Stark Young, who knew him well in the 1920's, has written:

> Sherwood Anderson was a combination, impossible to convey in words to anyone who never saw him, of the straightforward and contrived, of simple and disarming sincerity and elaborate, canny pose. . . . I was never sure when he was leaving off one and passing into the other; I am not sure he always knew himself when he was himself and when he was posing. I am speaking of something inner, far within, not merely of telling the truth. . . .

And Waldo Frank, in his memoir of Anderson, has recalled:

> At the time, when Anderson was about 40 and I was in my middle 20's, he personified for me the fecund sap of what he loved to call Mid-America. Anderson was a large man with a great surf of hair on his im-

pressive head. His features were broad, crude-cut like the not quite finished work of a genial wood-carver, yet exaggeratedly, almost femininely tender, and his eyes had both an animal distance and a depth of human subtlety and candor. His body, already somewhat soft, expressive of both grace and sensuous ease, was decked out in soft, expensive tweeds and mediterranean colors. . . . He would tell his tales (many of them never written) with an odd double-look in his eyes, as if one of them were wooing, the other sizing up.

Frank's last phrase is a striking summary of Anderson's post-*Winesburg* manner: one eye wooing, the other sizing up. In a few years this conflict in vision would result in a serious personal and literary crisis, but in the short stories he was now publishing in the magazines and in *Poor White*, the novel he published in 1920, his native tone of sweetness and realized love still came through clearly.

Although Anderson was not primarily a social novelist, his one novel dealing comprehensively with American society, *Poor White*, is remarkable for its avoidance of that split between humane ideology and aggressive power-hunger which disrupts the work of so many of his socially oriented contemporaries. Anderson may not have possessed a rightly disciplined mind, but the feeling he lodged at the center of *Poor White* seldom betrayed the story-pattern at its surface or the motivating ideas at its core. Whatever its structural weaknesses, the novel, at least in its first part, contains that rarity in American writing: integrated feeling.

Poor White may be divided into three parts: Books I and II describe the youth and early wanderings of Hugh McVey, a towering inarticulate Missouri boy who becomes a famous but still speechless inventor in Bidwell, Ohio; Book III is a sharp diversion to the girlhood and college days of Clara Butterworth, the daughter of a rich Bidwell farmer; and Books IV through VI bring the novel to an end in the courtship, marriage, unhappy marital life, and ultimate reconciliation of Hugh and Clara. By far the best part of the novel is the early story of Hugh McVey, which constitutes a beautifully proportioned portrait of the transition from the craftsman's town to the factory town in late-19th-century America. The remainder of *Poor White*, a study of disturbed sexuality, lacks the command of subject-matter found in the first two Books.

The opening pages of *Poor White* make one start with the realization of how enormous Mark Twain's influence has been on American writing. Hemingway's idiom, Faulkner's notion of Negro-white relations, Anderson's feeling for the American landscape can all be traced to Mark Twain. Anderson introduces Hugh McVey as the son of a tramp in "Mudcat Landing," a Missouri town along the Mississippi River, where father and son live in a fishing shack and the elder McVey drinks himself into a stupor. This scene immediately recalls the opening of *Huckleberry Finn* in which Huck, also the son of a drunken tramp, must find his way alone in the world. But where Mark Twain, writing in an idyllic vein about the pre-Civil War period, can let Huck drift down the Mississippi, away from society's pressures and secure in the affection of Nigger Jim, Anderson, writing more somberly about a far more somber period of American life, soon has Hugh working faithfully and dumbly in "Mudcat Landing." In the difference between these two opening scenes is mirrored a crucial transition in American life. Mark Twain's opening is more lively and inventive, but it is at least arguable that in the first few pages of *Poor White* Anderson has come close to him in sustaining a verbal tone which suggests the characteristic American landscape.

At the age of fourteen, "when the boy was on the point of sinking into the sort of animal-like stupor in which his father had lived," Hugh gets a job as a helper to a ticket-seller at the local railroad station. The ticket-seller's wife, Sarah Shepard, takes Hugh under her unexercised maternal wing: "She treated him like a child of six, told him how to sit at table, how to hold his fork when he ate. . . ." A New Englander to the core, Sarah "worked upon the problem of rooting the stupidity and dullness out of his mind as her father had worked at the problem of rooting the stumps out of the Michigan land."

Here Anderson has hewn one of his fundamental situations: the dumb giant erupting from stupor into sensibility. Hugh McVey, the tongue-tied boy who must force himself to stay awake and not relapse into the sweet sleep of a Missouri summer day, will pull down the pastoral society he mutely loves and construct another from which he is to be forever alienated. This bumbling small-town Ishmael is craned from his sloth by a life-hungry woman who personifies the mores of the commercial East; but after Hugh has helped make Bidwell into a factory town which is the material realization of Sarah Shepard's values, he is more homeless than ever. Whether Anderson was aware of the historical pertinence of this fable to the development of American industrial society hardly matters: it is there and it is right.

In the opening section of *Poor White* Anderson uses no dialogue at all, which is a happy choice not merely because he lacked the gift for composing individualized conversation but also because the writing at this point is neither dramatic nor what could properly be called fictional narrative. As in most of his best work, Anderson is here employing the tone of controlled reminiscence, low-pitched and subdued, full of notes of near-silence to suggest a lost past. Here is a characteristic sentence, a blend of the vernacular with conscious rhetorical devices: "The soil, yellow, shallow and stony, was tilled, in Hugh's time, by a race of long gaunt men who seemed as exhausted and no-account as the land on which they lived." The phrase "no-account" comes as a distinct surprise, a touch of common speech in a finely molded sentence; a considerable risk but a successfully negotiated one.

Like Mark Twain before him, Anderson uses the Mississippi as a symbolic presence to suggest the strength, contentment, and silence for which his central character yearns. Twain: "When it was dark I set by my campfire smoking and feeling pretty satisfied, but by and by it got sort of lonesome, and so I went and set on the bank and listened to the current swashing along and counted the stars and drift-logs and rafts that came down and then went to bed; there ain't no better way to put in time when you are lonesome. . . ." Anderson: "Above his head a breeze played through the branches of the trees, and insects sang in the grass. Everything about him was clean. A lovely stillness pervaded the river and the woods. He lay on his belly and gazed down over the river out of sleep-heavy eyes into hazy distances." Admittedly, the Twain passage, if only because it is so much less "literary," is the better of the two—but then there have been few American writers who could match the beauty of such passages in *Huckleberry Finn*. What is important, however, in this comparison is the continuity of feeling between the two writers, a continuity based at least as much on similarity of response as on literary adaptation.

Perhaps most valuable in these early chapters of *Poor White* is their authenticity as a portrait of late-19th-century American life. As Hugh McVey wanders eastward in search of "the place where happiness was to come to him," he finds only the self-centered agitation that stirs the industrial towns. "Hugh looked at the people who were whirling along past him, and shivered with the nameless fear . . . [of] country boys in the city." In one town Hugh notices the external signs of the new way of life: "Although it was nearly ten o'clock when he arrived, people still walked about in the streets and many stores were open." It is a time of restless stirring, a time in which "thought and poetry passed away. . . . Serious young men in Bidwell . . . whose fathers had walked together on moonlight nights along Turner's Pike to talk of God, went away to technical schools." In Chapter XI of the novel Anderson has written a series of remarkable vignettes of Bidwell's people, showing how changes in the town's economy affect their lives. Sam Hunter, a shrewd speculator, attaches himself to Hugh and makes a fortune out of his genius; Tom Butterworth, a farmer, hardens under the temptation of money; and Joe Wainsworth, a harness maker, is pathetically unable to understand that his craftsman's approach to work is becoming obsolete. The Wainsworth episode suggests the grotesquerie of *Winesburg*, and, though poorly integrated into the novel's structure, is the most effective piece of writing in *Poor White.*

Near Bidwell Hugh finds a job as a telegraph operator in a small railroad station. He is filled with "a hungry desire to enter the lives of the people about him," but almost like the king of a primitive tribe bound to isolation by ritual, he is destined, as the hero who will transform Bidwell's life, to remain alone. "He wanted to . . . be the friend of people whose lives were beautifully lived and who were themselves beautiful and full of significance." But instead he acquires the reputation in Bidwell of being a strange and hence a deep one. He walks in the streets, this hulking man-child, and is watched with awe, for surely a man so inaccessible, so seemingly self-contained must be thinking deep thoughts. To keep his mind from rotting Hugh sets himself to doing meaningless tasks, counting the trees along a street and cutting off great armfuls of twigs which he carries to his room and weaves into a basket. This is one of Anderson's most magnificent symbolic touches—the figure of a man yearning for community yet able to ward off madness only by the uncreative weaving of twigs into an unwanted basket. It is a symbolic version of Anderson's recurrent theme that "all men lead their lives in silence behind a wall of misunderstanding . . . and most men die in silence and unnoticed behind the walls." This is a notion that could flourish only in a culture deeply ridden by a sense of alienation; a notion that, in one way or another, has absorbed the imagination of most major American writers.

Driven increasingly inward (we are never quite certain whether his muteness derives from some inherent per-

sonal failing or from the pressures of society), Hugh turns
to inventing machines, and thereby transforms the quality
of Bidwell's life. Men who had once noticed the "sweet
smell of new-cut pine boards" now work till midnight
over their accounts. "The cry, 'Get on in the world,' that
rang all over America . . . rang in the streets of Bidwell." Though finally a wealthy and famous man, Hugh
remains locked behind the walls of his self.

In *Poor White* Anderson has given untainted expression to the persistent American myth of loneliness, according to which power is punished by isolation: the society that has made money its dominant objective indicates its self-doubt and guilt by stubbornly insisting that
the wealthy are unhappy; the society that believes, as no
other, in success yet feels a need to brand it with disap-
proval. Hugh McVey, combining two main constituents
of American character, Ford's mindless inventiveness and
Lincoln's lonely brooding, has been driven to his work
largely by the barrenness of his life; which is to say that
the rise of American industrial society is the culmination
of a previous failure in sociality and that in such a society
work is intimately related to the absence of creative activity.
The central symbol of the book, through which it gains a
quality of muted pathos, is the basket woven in desperation:
the basket that is neither product nor commodity but token
of despair.

Once its focus of attention shifts from Hugh, *Poor
White* quickly declines in interest. The story of Clara
Butterworth splits the book in half, a wound never quite
healed. Clara's sexual problems, her relations with a les-
bian, her decision to marry Hugh because he is like "an
honest, powerful horse," fall somewhere between the

mildly ridiculous and the barely plausible; they lack the knowing certainty of representation that fortifies the first part of *Poor White*. Anderson is invariably better when he can write as a chronicler of his people's fate than when he screws himself up to write as a problem novelist. Most unsatisfactory is the book's ending in which, through some vague gesture of coupling, Hugh and Clara are supposed to find each other. Anderson has not allowed Hugh's internal drive to self-defeat to reach its necessary end and, through a curious aversion to dramatic conflict, has failed to bring Hugh and Clara into the expected and necessary confrontation.

Poor White does not succeed in becoming a unified narrative: it lacks enough directly visualized action to drive to a dramatic climax, it is very hazy about time progressions, and its two major themes, though not necessarily unrelated, are never welded together. But its first part remains one of the most beautiful and significant pieces of American imaginative prose. Here Anderson speaks clearly and movingly in his own voice, the voice of the bardic chronicler. As Hugh McVey is a figure profoundly involved in the American experience, so Anderson's prose is dipped deeply into the flavors of American speech. From *Poor White* there emerges an imaginative version of American society at its late-19th-century turning-point which other writers have equaled or surpassed in acuity but none in blending acuity with a uniquely tender nostalgia.

The critical response to *Poor White* was as warm as it should have been. Robert Morss Lovett did a favorable review in *The Dial*, the best literary journal in America during the early 1920's, and Frank and Rosenfeld praised the book in public print and private letters. (All three saw, however, the book's central weakness: Frank noted that Anderson "never really fleshed the relationship [Hugh and Clara] must after all have had;" Rosenfeld wrote in a letter that "The cut-backs in *Poor White*, I must confess, annoyed me very much"; and Lovett perceptively remarked in his review that the book "does not end—it merely stops.") Within his narrow limits Huebsch pushed the book commercially, and a year after its publication it had sold slightly under 3200 copies.

All of which was gratifying to Anderson; but the very gratification only intensified his yearning to move eastward, to New York and beyond. When the generous-souled Paul Rosenfeld wired Anderson in January 1921 offering to pay his passage for a trip to Europe, Anderson replied, "This year it has been very hard for me to live in the Middle-West. I can come back here to live but I have been deeply hungry to go into old cities, see old cultural things. You have opened the door for me. . . . O, Paul, I can't tell you what this chance and the opportunity it offers for companionship with you means to me."

In May of that year Anderson, Tennessee, and Rosenfeld sailed for Paris, where they stayed through the summer. For Anderson it was an exciting experience: he loved Paris with total sensuous abandonment, the city seemed to him to represent in color and movement all that old-world culture should. The journalist Lewis Galantière, who had known Anderson in Chicago and was now working in Paris, guided the visitors through Paris and to the Cathedral of Chartres before which Anderson stood deeply impressed. Now at the peak of his powers

both as writer and as person, and colorfully dressed in
loose tweeds with a bright silk handkerchief knotted as a
tie, Anderson delighted in walking the Parisian streets,
grasping impressions, observing scenes, and chatting to
strangers in a blend of French, English, and finger-signs.
Paul Rosenfeld was later to recall:

> Sherwood was overwrought on our first day in Paris.
> Crossing the court of the Tuileries with him I fancied
> he'd gotten a cinder in his eye, so vehemently was he
> rubbing the organ. He turned aside, leaned an arm on
> the pedestal of a statue. It was tears. "I have never
> thought anything on earth could be so beautiful!" he
> stammered. . . .

Anderson's most important visit in Paris was to
Gertrude Stein. These two shrewd Americans understood
each other perfectly, loved to swap stories, and respected
each other's gift for shaping language. In *The Autobiography of Alice B. Toklas* Gertrude Stein has inimitably
described Anderson's visit:

> For some reason or other I [Alice Toklas] was not
> present on this occasion, some domestic complication
> in all probability, at any rate when I did come home
> Gertrude Stein was moved and pleased as she has
> very rarely been. Gertrude Stein was in those days a
> little bitter, all her unpublished manuscripts, and no
> hope of publication or serious recognition. Sherwood
> Anderson came and quite simply and directly as is his
> way told her what he thought of her work and what it
> had meant to him in his development. He told it to her
> then and what was even rarer he told it in print im-
> mediately after. Gertrude Stein and Sherwood Ander-
> son have always been the best of friends, but I do not
> believe even he realizes how much his visit meant to
> her.

They remained friends for the rest of their lives. A few months after returning to America, Anderson sent her a note introducing a young man "instinctively in touch with everything worth while going on here," Ernest Hemingway. In 1922 Anderson did his warm introduction to *Geography and Plays,* and in the same year he wrote to his brother Karl his more intimate and balanced opinion of Stein's work: "As for Stein I do not think her too important. I do think she had an important thing to do, not for the public but for the artist who happens to work with words as his material." Which is as good a capsule appraisal of Stein as anyone is likely to write.

It was inconceivable to Anderson that, after Paris, he could return to advertising copy and Chicago. For several months he worked in New York as a "publicity man" with an independent movie company in which his boyhood friend, John Emerson, was an executive. The job was pretty much of a sinecure, as Emerson intended it to be, but it could not last long; by the end of 1921 Anderson was unemployed, with only advertising in Chicago open to him. But to that he refused to return, and from early 1922 until the summer of 1926, when he built his house in Virginia, Anderson was to wander across the country, living in New York, Chicago, Reno, New Orleans, and Berkeley. Through most of his life he was a restless wanderer, drifting from place to place in search of something he could hardly have named but which was perhaps a sense of home. During the five years between his first trip to Paris and the building of the house, Anderson's life was particularly unsettled: his reputation was growing but the first puzzling and painful critical attacks on his more recent and "contemporaneous" work were beginning to appear; the problem of money irked him intermittently; and his personal life, particularly his relations with his friends and his wife, was beset by frequent crises.

Anderson kept publishing a book each year. In 1921 came *Triumph of the Egg,* 1922-23 *Many Marriages,* 1923 *Horses and Men,* 1924 *A Story Teller's Story,* and in 1925 *Dark Laughter.* The two volumes of stories, which contained some of his best work, were well received; his autobiographical volume appealed to the mood of the early 1920's; and the two novels, while both inferior work, sold well, *Dark Laughter* becoming, in fact, Anderson's only "best-seller." *Winesburg* was included in the Modern Library reprint series in 1922 and sold as much in its first month as it had in the first year of its original edition. Anderson could not yet earn a comfortable living from his writings, but it seemed to him that he soon might.

The serious reader whose taste has been molded by the literary standards of the 1940's, and who is too young to remember the 1920's as a personal experience, is not likely to realize the extent of Anderson's reputation at the time. To say that cultivated readers of the early 1920's admired his work as highly as such readers today admire Faulkner's is to exaggerate only a little. No other American novelist appeared so frequently in *The Dial,* a review of greater influence than any subsequent American literary journal. His work was analyzed in a great many critical articles, most of them favorable. *The Literary Digest,* the *Time* of its day, gave its readers a "take-out" of his personality. In December 1921 *The Dial* presented him with the first of its annual $2,000 awards. And a few years later Virginia Woolf could report in *The Saturday Review of Literature* that "Of all American novelists the most discussed and read in England at the present moment are probably Mr. Sherwood Anderson and Mr. Sinclair Lewis." Of all these signs of esteem, the most significant was the *Dial* award, and perhaps the best measure of its significance is the fact that the second recipient of the award was T. S. Eliot.

The homage he received in the early 1920's Anderson did not take with quite adequate grace and ease; he was not prepared to. Though claiming to disdain the more fashionable areas of the New York literary world, he was yet gratified and a little "taken in" when he found himself circled by admirers at cocktail parties. Waldo Frank has recalled these years with a not unsympathetic penetration:

> Although he [Anderson] respected the "East," he was quite ready to take it on, and to take it over. His confidence was not as cunning as he supposed. Subtly at first, the East invaded him and began to blur the lines of his inward integration. And long before the shattering trials and challenges of the 1930's, Sherwood Anderson had become confused—had become a variant of his own creations.
>
> Sensing this, he tried to escape—to Virginia, to New Orleans. But the confusion went with him. . . . He would spend hours with people who lionized him, and whom he said he despised, and be ashamed to mention where he had been.

Frank's picture is essentially correct, but it does tend somewhat to the sentimental view that Anderson was a "whole" and pure-souled Midwestern pagan until corrupted by the evil, sophisticated East. This view has been rather curiously shared by those eastern intellectuals who romanticized Anderson and those of his Chicago friends in whom jealousy and a willed sectional provincialism made it only too easy for them to blame his later difficulties on the East. As should by now be clear, these difficulties were deeply lodged in his character; they partly derived from his upbringing, his education, and his need to relate himself securely to the intellectuals; and while they may have been aggravated in New York they had already become evident in Chicago.

That there was a certain blurring, a "softening" of Anderson's personality in the early 1920's is undeniable. It came through in touches of artiness: a readiness to declaim about "the Artist" in the cadence of self-consciousness, a somewhat primitivistic attempt to dress in gaudy colors, and a straining after elegant "effortless" style in his writing. It came through also in his increasing sensitivity to criticism, his burning long and sore when *The Dial* ran an obtuse attack on him by Alyse Gregory. What saved him, what kept him from hurtling into a crackup was that, as a man who enjoyed watching himself play a social role, he could see the many tempting roads to self-destruction. To Paul Rosenfeld he wrote in 1922: "As to the matter of my going to pieces . . . what I think is that I have allowed people to make me a bit too conscious of myself." If part of him succumbed to public temptations, another and healthier part of him kept trying to escape them.

Perhaps the reason for Anderson's confused relation to "the East" was that even as he absorbed so many of its dominant values he could never quite feel at home in it. A man who thinks of himself as in some sense a folk-spokesman is not likely to be satisfied with literary cocktail parties, social lionizing, and hotel sojourns, no matter how pleasant they may temporarily seem. Anderson had sought out the cultural fleshpots of the big city, but susceptible though he was to their delights he yet heeded the voice in the depths of his mind that told him to learn what he could—and flee.

In the 1920's literary New York represented an inter-regnum between two coercive historical pressures: unlike the Chicago of 1912, it no longer needed to devote it-self to sloughing off the small town—that is, to discarding a constrictive strand of the American past; and unlike itself of a decade later, it was not yet burdened by the incubus of Europe—that is, by a consciousness of the decay of the capitalist present. The young writers who began to appear in print in the 1920's were privileged to feel a sense of social elbow-room at least as great as that felt during the "Chicago Renaissance," while at the same time they could play with a slightly cynical and, in many instances, boyishly innocent cosmopolitanism that was quite beyond the earlier Chicago writers. The New York literary world of the 1920's was a successor to the Chicago of the previous decade, but it had an ease, a polish, and a sophistication the young provincials in Chicago could neither achieve nor simulate.

America itself in the 1920's was at last an acknowl-edged great power, a creditor nation gradually putting Europe, as Trotsky quipped, on rations; there was money in the New York air and a bright young writer might siphon some of it into his pocket. Politics seemed not, as the intellectuals of the 1940's would come to feel, disreputable or amoral, but rather boring, the preoccupation of men who were puritans, philistines, or prigs. Ideas were treated with cavalier leniency, for the consequences of mishandling them were not too immediately painful. Yet the 1920's were not quite the "Jazz Age" Fitzgerald has made them seem, and those who accept his nostalgic recollections at face value will get a slightly distorted view of the period; there was plenty of serious work being done and there was certainly a startling amount of talent, there was a willingness to take chances with work and careers that somewhat compensated for intellectual carelessness, and there was rather more substance to life than Fitzgerald's glossy version of it might suggest. Between the 1920's and all subsequent periods of American intellectual life there is this crucial difference: its participants could feel the presence of a "margin," mistakes didn't have to be fatal, the world could still be kept at a distance, and for creative work risks were gladly assumed. But if the 1920's were not quite what Fitzgerald thought they were, they must nonetheless seem an entirely different world from what later generations have known, and perhaps the particular poignancy felt in Fitzgerald's writing is due to his having expressed the clearest and often callowest version of the 1920's' *Zeitgeist* while simultaneously anticipating the oncoming catastrophe.

The key word was freedom. To a writer like Sherwood Anderson the 1920's created an atmosphere of freedom in at least three senses. The persistent campaign, and sometimes cant, directed against "puritanism," the theme of self-realization that Anderson had first celebrated in

Chicago, the credulous expectation that without regard for a limiting social context one could escape and then again escape to some new and grander shore of personal freedom—these were the notes struck in heavy chorus during the 1920's, the decade when Anderson began to write fiction with "contemporary" settings. But in the literary life of the 'twenties there was another and more immediately accessible freedom which Anderson respected and which there is still reason to respect. Among the young writers in New York there was often a lighthearted and chivalrous fraternity, a generosity that came from self-assurance and swirling hopes; a willingness, too, to accept differences of taste as a natural and pleasing condition. The literary polemics, such as the famous skirmish over Dadaism, were conducted in a spirit of gaiety that the contentious 'thirties and lugubrious 'forties could not have summoned. Not that the writers who flourished in the 1920's were conspicuously "better" people than those of later decades; it was rather that life was better to them and they could therefore be good to each other. Today the reader who intensely admires Fitzgerald's work is not likely to admire Anderson's, but that sort of polarization of taste did not seem necessary in the 1920's. Fitzgerald himself felt, as he told Edmund Wilson and John Dos Passos, that Anderson was "a wonder."

To Anderson the 1920's suggested freedom in still another sense: he associated it with the waste and wildness of cosmopolitan life. Tempted though he was by that life, Anderson repeatedly withdrew from it, sensing perhaps that the roots of his creativity could find nourishment only in other soils. That he could always contrive a retreat from the big city was his particular good fortune and very possibly the one thing which saved him from the kind of disaster that overwhelmed Fitzgerald.

Immediately after winning the *Dial* award Anderson left New York to live in New Orleans for several months. The $2,000 would enable him to write uninterruptedly for a year, Tennessee was in Chicago busy with her own affairs, his advertising work seemed less and less tolerable, he had begun to suffer from chronic colds during the winter months, and he wanted to observe the life of the southern Negro—these were among his reasons for moving south.

It was a happy move. Since early 1921 there had been published in New Orleans a literary monthly, *The Double Dealer*, around which clustered a group of rather lively young intellectuals. Anderson soon befriended these people and found them both pleasant and stimulating: they satisfied his need to be with intellectuals and yet were not so overpowering as to make him feel insecure. He became a frequent contributor to *The Double Dealer*, particularly since it was more receptive than most magazines to the prose-poems he later collected in *A New Testament*.

Living in a rather dilapidated rooming house in the French quarter, Anderson indulged his love for colorful dress and an easy-going manner of life. In the mornings he would work on his novel *Many Marriages*, and then he would loll about the city for the rest of the day, wandering through the dock section where he liked to talk to people and watch the Negro stevedores at work. As William Faulkner was to conclude when he met Anderson in 1924, this was indeed a pleasant way to live. Seldom before and probably never afterwards did Anderson feel so radiant and vigorous, so ready to forget for the moment the personal and career troubles associated with Chicago and New York. When the Mardi Gras was held he threw himself into it with a rich zest, joining the parade and returning to a party of his friends with an enlarged repertoire of off-color songs.

Julius Friend, editor of *The Double Dealer*, has recalled Anderson's appearance when he first visited the magazine's office: "He was an exotic spectacle! His long hair fell in strands over his florid face. His apparel: a rough tweed suit with leather buttons, a loud tie on which was strung a large paste finger ring, red socks with yellow bands, a velour hat with a red feather stuck in it. He carried a heavy blackthorn stick." But though he affected a burlesque-show version of a racing tout's dress, Anderson had little interest in race tracks themselves; when Friend took him once he seemed bored and out of place. Anderson's dress, his interest in women and in Negroes, his liking for the odd corners of New Orleans, were less spontaneous responses to actual moments of his experience than symbols of a rebellion against the standardization and abstraction of American urban life; he was searching for saving remnants of values that were rapidly being destroyed.

In March 1922 Anderson reluctantly left New Orleans for Chicago, telling his friends that he had to mend his fences, which meant to wind up his advertising affairs and, one might add without malice, his marriage. A few months later he went to New York, where he spent the summer in Ben Huebsch's apartment. In August he was writing to Gertrude Stein, "I have run away from all my friends, including friend wife. . . ."

Anderson's marriage, marked by long separations and casual encounters, had always been a distinctly haphazard affair. At first Tennessee had satisfied his image of the intellectual woman, but soon Anderson realized that the image was rather flat. Tennessee's decidedly unfeminine austerity tended to impress but even more to chill men; in character she was rather like Anderson's mother, and though this similarity was enough to have once made her seem attractive, it could hardly keep him a devoted, let alone passionate, husband. Whenever she could come close enough, Tennessee made the mistake of trying to dominate him, and though Anderson wanted the kind of woman who could "manage" his life for him, he also wanted one who had enough tact to know the difference between "managing" and dominating. What most annoyed him, however, was Tennessee's increasing ambition in his behalf: she wanted him to become a worldly "success," she tried to get him to wear full-dress to the opera while she sported a lorgnette, and she urged him to read *Death in Venice* as a model for the cultivated style she hoped he would develop.

Disorganized in his personal life and unable to do much serious work, Anderson remained in New York until the spring of 1923. *Many Marriages*, which then seemed so bold a novel that it was subjected to under-the-counter restrictions by a few wholesale book companies, brought in enough money to allow him another year of unmolested literary work. Marking time in New York, Anderson met and apparently fell in love with Elizabeth Prall, a young woman who managed Lord & Taylor's bookshop.

When he left for Reno in the spring of 1923 to divorce Tennessee, it was understood that he would soon marry Elizabeth Prall.

It took Anderson almost a year to get his divorce, for despite the fact that the marriage had never been very successful Tennessee bitterly resisted ending it. She had been gradually discovering that the role of the "new woman" left her unsatisfied, that her feelings for Anderson were growing deeper than she had expected them to, and that the thought of again being "independent" was thoroughly frightening. In view of her proclaimed opinions she could hardly fall back on the line that she refused to give up her husband because she loved him, truth though that would have been; she had therefore to resort to pathetic stratagems in order to hinder the divorce proceedings. As Anderson rather cruelly wrote to his brother Karl in early 1924, "Apparently all her talk about feminism was for others." Tennessee agreed to the divorce only after Anderson's Chicago friend, the historian Ferdinand Schevill, teased her into admitting that she, of all people, could hardly refuse freedom to a man who wanted it.

While living in Reno Anderson wrote a book of reminiscences, *A Story Teller's Story*, which appeared in 1924. Though praised even by critics indifferent to most of Anderson's work, *A Story Teller's Story* is false in its feeling, its thought, and its composition. Purporting to be a free autobiography, the book is neither record nor fiction, loyal neither to fact nor to imagination. It contains untruths which cannot be excused merely by saying that Anderson was uninterested in facts: e.g., "in all my life I have never for a moment subscribed to the philosophy

of life as set forth in the *Saturday Evening Post.*" Its tone
is a mixture of self-indulgence and accommodation: the
former in its wispy objectless musings and the latter in
its grossly sentimentalized version of Anderson's life
which so satisfied "sophisticated" readers of the 1920's.
(Anderson's father, so brutally portrayed in *Windy Mc-
Pherson's Son,* was now transformed into a sort of native
jolly gleeman.) What is most false about the book is
that Anderson, conforming to the coziest American non-
conformism, depicted himself exactly as his readers
expected him to be. He absorbed into his autobiography
the most pervasive patterns of American mythology: the
poverty-stricken childhood, the troubled adolescence, the
struggle for "success" and the struggle to resist it, the
brooding concern for the fate of the nation. Of all his
books *A Story Teller's Story* is least related to the reality
of particularized recollection or imaginative creation; it
is a work, as he says, of "the fancy." Viewed in terms of
Anderson's literary development, the book seems most
important for its abandonment of his native style. The
prose lacks the clumsy angularity of his earlier books,
but it thereby also lacks their strength and tension; it is
a prose as boneless and slippery as a piece of raw liver,
and to a disastrous extent it is a prose designed to ingra-
tiate.

In April 1924, directly after his divorce from Tennessee, Anderson married Elizabeth Prall. That summer they
went to live in New Orleans, but it was no longer the
joyous New Orleans Anderson had known two years earlier: *The Double Dealer* was dying, its editors turning
to jobs and careers. While in New Orleans Anderson met

William Faulkner and for a short time the two men were close friends. With his canny insight into prospective talent, Anderson encouraged Faulkner to write and helped get his first novel published. The two men would meet in the afternoons and evenings, talking and drinking, exchanging the tall tales they both loved, and once quarreling over the absurd question of whether Negroes and whites could interbreed indefinitely. (Anderson said yes.) The relationship soon chilled, partly because of the quarrel and partly because Faulkner parodied Anderson's style in an introduction he wrote for a local artist's book of drawings. But the two men always felt a lingering, distant respect for each other: Anderson admired Faulkner's virtuosity, and in his inept novel *Mosquitoes* Faulkner drew a portrait of Anderson that was slightly satiric but mainly affectionate.

Perhaps the main difficulty in Anderson's stay in New Orleans was that his third marriage showed few signs of being any more successful than his previous two. He had married Cornelia Lane when she seemed to him a personification of well-bred comfort; he had married Tennessee Mitchell when she seemed to him the epitome of independence and rebelliousness; and now, when he was greatly attracted by what might be called established culture, he was married to Elizabeth Prall. In a letter sent to his brother Karl, he referred respectfully to Elizabeth's "gentle aristocracy," a phrase that sums up his vision of her. (Faulkner, who may have intended something more than Southern gallantry, always called her "Miss Elizabeth.") She was a tiny woman devoid of conspicuous attractions, who came from a gentle and possibly overrefined academic family, and while she admired Anderson a great deal she seems also to have felt a need to make his unpolished genius acceptable to the more genteel reader. She persuaded him to tone down his resplendent clothes, she made him keep regular hours, she had him take her to a New Orleans country club and be photographed together with Dorothy Dix—and for a while he obeyed. Elizabeth Prall was a fine woman, but hardly the sort who could remain married very long to Sherwood Anderson.

Until the summer of 1926, when the heat drove him northward, Anderson continued to live in New Orleans. For some years now he had been wandering about the country, unable to find a permanent home. His life had been marked by alternations between periods of exuberant confidence and gloomy insecurity. To support himself he had begun taking lecture trips in 1925, a business he found extremely distasteful. Now almost 50 years old, Anderson was no more secure or "settled" than a young unknown writer. He could not earn his living from his serious writings, his reputation was being called into question by the critics and by the appearance of younger rivals like Faulkner and Hemingway, and he himself was becoming increasingly uncertain of his talent. He was in a crisis that was to continue for at least several years and perhaps until the end of his life.

The Short Stories

ALTHOUGH there is a gap of more than a decade between Anderson's first two volumes of stories and his last one, chronology is of slight consequence to a study of his career as a story writer. *Death in the Woods*, which appeared in 1933, contains a few stories quite different in style and subject matter from those in the earlier books, but except for one or two sketches of Southern hillsmen none of these later innovations is particularly important. The one significant line of division in his stories cuts equally through all three books.

Some eight or ten of Anderson's stories, by far the best he ever wrote, can be considered a coherent group. Such stories as "I Want to Know Why," "The Egg," "Death in the Woods," "I'm a Fool," "The Man Who Became a Woman," and to a lesser extent "The Corn Planting," "A Meeting South," and "Brother Death" are similar in having as their structural base an oral narration, as their tone a slightly bewildered tenderness, and as their subject matter elemental crises in the lives of simple townspeople. In these stories the central figure is often an "I" who stands at the rim of the action, sometimes looking back to his boyhood and remembering an incident he now realizes to have been crucial to his life, a moment in which he took one of those painful leaps that climax the process of growth. The narrator tells his story in a manner that is an implicit rejection of literary naturalism: he cannot content himself with a catalogue of behavior for he realizes that in the word "behavior" are coiled the greatest enigmas; he stresses the strangeness of his remembered experience because he feels that the ordinary can best be perceived through the intense light cast by the strange; and though he now claims a partial understanding of the incident that persists in his memory, that understanding is itself a humility before the general problem of human experience. Life, as he conceives it, is buried in marshes of sloth and apathy, and only in a rare emergence into awareness does one find its epiphany, the *true moment.*

Anderson's narrator senses that in the seemingly simple act of telling his story he enters into a highly complex relation with his audience and that, as one able to shape both the materials of his narrative and the responses of his listeners, he is momentarily in a position of great power. The atmosphere of oral narration, deliberately created by Anderson, is the setting of his best stories, which can be read not merely as imaginative versions of human experience but as renderings of a pervasive pattern of story-telling. Part of the craft of oral narration consists in the narrator's working not only for the usual kinds of interest and suspense, but also to produce in his listeners a vicarious responsibility for the successful completion of the story. The audience quickly senses this relationship and, if the narrator is at all skilled, becomes emotionally involved with his struggle to tell his story almost as much as with the story itself.

The narrator is seen weighing his recollection in his mind, perplexed by the course it has taken and wondering whether it is merely of private significance or of larger emblematic value. As he turns to the memory that is his burden, he seems doubtful that he will be able to extract it from the chaos of the past and give it form. He becomes aware, as well, of the temptations that follow from his power as story teller, but it is a particular virtue of Anderson's short fictions that his narrator does not try to dominate or assert superiority over his audience. Respecting the community of narrator and listener, or writer and reader, Anderson establishes as his controlling point of view the voice of a hesitant human being, one who is anything but omniscient.

In choosing to simulate oral narrative Anderson was aware of the traditional resources he could thereby tap. Sensing that story-telling had once been a ceremony in which the listeners expected the narrator thoroughly to exploit his craft and thus fulfill his communal role, Anderson quite cannily tried to re-establish something of this atmosphere of ritual in his stories. He hoped to lend the act of story-telling a synoptic significance it could not otherwise have, to restore to the story teller a fraction of his role as tribal spokesman or, at least, public figure. But he also sensed, as had Conrad before him, that the most effective story teller is one who is felt to be not merely skillful but also deeply involved in the outcome of his own story. The Andersonian narrator therefore seeks to persuade his audience that the disburdening of his mind has a purpose other than the stimulation of its pleasure; he hints that for him, and perhaps through him for the audience, the recollection of the past provides an occasion for a symbolic cleansing and relief. And, in more private terms, he would certainly have agreed with D. H. Lawrence that "One sheds one's sickness in books—repeats and presents again one's emotions to be master of them."

In those of his stories that follow the oral narrative pattern, Anderson often resorts to a bold sort of artlessness. The narrator of "The Egg," for example, occasionally confesses his perplexity before the events he recalls. Such an intrusion of comment into a narrative is considered a heresy, or at least a fallacy, by certain severe critics; and, indeed, by derailing the story from its guiding point of view an intrusion can immediately destroy every shred of verisimilitude. But in those of Anderson's stories that live, artlessness is usually the veil of conscious craft, and the narrator's intrusion, precisely because it *is* the narrator's and not Anderson's, becomes an integral part of the story. Even while wandering from his narrative line, the oral story teller will drive his apparent divagations toward his climax—and this is exactly the strategy Anderson employs.

It is interesting that the untutored listener will often have a greater regard for this element of narrative contrivance than the sophisticated reader who has been educated to expect "naturalness" in art. The untutored listener realizes that he is supposed to discount, though not disregard, the narrator's claim to be baffled by his own story, for that claim is part of his craft. (This is particularly noticeable in an audience listening to a ghost story.) The listener instinctively senses what the modern critic strives to restate as doctrine: a story, being primarily a story, is not reproducible in any terms but its own, and after the work of exegesis is done there still remains a dimension of unexplicated wonder, to which the story teller will naturally direct his awe and thereby the audience's attention. The narrative device that might be called the protestation to perplexity is a traditional and almost an instinctive way of telling a story, used by Homer and Defoe, Conrad and Twain.

But it is the mark of the good story teller that, even as he confesses to bewilderment about the story's meaning, he is actually presenting the reader with the materials necessary for a total response. Sometimes, as in "The Egg," both Anderson and his narrator seem slightly bewildered by the story's terrible events, but the story is nevertheless there in its entirety and virtual perfection. Sometimes, as in "Death in the Woods," the narrator confesses that "the notes had to be picked up slowly one at a time," but Anderson himself has them all firmly in possession and control. In either instance, all that is important is that the reader not feel that he has been unduly deprived or overloaded; and there is surely no warrant for either feeling with regard to "The Egg" or "Death in the Woods."

A great deal of cant has been written to the effect that Anderson's stories are "moving" but "formless"—as if a work of art could be moving unless it were formed or form could have any end other than to move. Those who make such remarks are taking form to signify merely the executive plan or technical devices that go into the making of a work of art. But while form includes these it is not reducible to them—unless, of course, one prefers to take the scaffolding as the purpose of the construction. In modern literary discussion form is too often seen as a virtually autonomous and isolable characteristic of a work of art, too often equated with the conscious planning of a James or the elaborate structure of a Proust. And when one tends to think of form largely in terms of the complex and elaborate, one may soon deny it to the simple and primitive. Actually, however, form can be properly apprehended only by relating techniques and strategies to their organic context of emotion and theme, and it is consequently difficult to imagine a work of art with acknowledged authenticity of emotion to be simultaneously lacking in form. Valuable and finely formed fictions, such as some of Anderson's stories and Lawrence's novels, result not merely from the contrivance of skilled intention but also from the flow of released unconscious materials—which is to be taken not as a plea against the use of the blue pencil but as a statement of what it is used on.

In Anderson's best stories, form is achieved through two essential means: tone and perspective. Tone is the outward sign of the emotion resident in a work of art; it is the essence of what a writer communicates, undercutting and simultaneously uniting subject matter and character portrayal. The tone of love, as realized in the best stories and in *Winesburg*, is the ultimate quality for which Anderson should be read. One reason this tone is so fully present in his best stories is that the structure of the oral narrative, while itself simple, yet permits him a perspective on his material that is both consistent and complex. The consistency is largely derived from his use of the first person as narrator, while the complexity is enforced by an interaction of the four levels of movement in his stories: the events themselves; the feelings of the boy involved in them; the memory of the adult who weighs his involvement in the light of accumulated experience; and the final increment of meaning suggested by the story but beyond the conscious recognition of its narrator. The true action of these stories is thus not the events narrated but the narrator's response, not the perceived object but the perceiving subject. That is why Anderson's stories are so seldom dramatic in the usual sense of the term: their purpose is not to record a resolution of conflict but to refract an enlargement of consciousness.

Somewhat less complex than this abstract model of Anderson's "oral" narratives are his two most popular stories, "I'm a Fool" and "I Want to Know Why." Though both are written in the first person, their narrators speak, not as men looking back to boyhood, but as boys involved in the immediate present. The result is a rich quality of sensuousness, but also an absence of the irony and complication of vision possible in the stories where the narrator is an adult.

Anderson himself sensed that neither story could be considered in the same class as "The Egg" or "The Man Who Became a Woman," and of the excessively ingenuous "I'm a Fool" he wrote to Van Wyck Brooks that "its wide acceptance is largely due to the fact that it is a story of immaturity and poses no problem." "I'm a Fool" and "I Want to Know Why" are usually taken to be quite similar stories, perhaps because both are dramatic monologues of racetrack swipes, but actually the difference between them is so considerable that to specify it is to begin a properly discriminating judgment of Anderson's work as a story writer.

In intention "I'm a Fool" is patterned after Mark Twain, but in execution it is closer to Tarkington. The monologue of the boy who outsmarts himself through an excess of shrewdness is internally coherent and only occasionally disrupted by "literary" phrasing. But this coherence is not related to the boy himself; the monologue is inconceivable from the lips of "a big lumbering fellow of nineteen" who has learned to drink and "swear from fellows who know how." The surface of his musing is too coy for the character it is supposed to reflect, and no attribution of ironic intent can dispel the incongruity. Actually, the monologue comes from Anderson's own mouth, Sherwood masquerading as an adolescent in "dirty horsey pants" and improvising a remarkable imitation of adolescent reverie—while pointing with the elbows of his prose to how ingenious an act it is. Too ambitious in motivation to be taken as the ironic anecdote it might have been, "I'm a Fool" is insufficiently ambitious in execution to be a very good story. The boy's unhappiness is too local to what is merely adolescent in his experience, and hence cannot thoroughly involve the reader to whom the significance of adolescence is in its tension of "becoming."

This is precisely the effect Anderson does achieve in "I Want to Know Why," also a story in which an adolescent narrator describes a troubling experience at a race track. In the story's rambling opening, the boy is revealed through several neatly economical touches; he is "just crazy" about horses and he feels a strong sense of companionship with the Negro swipes. In the boy's feeling there is clearly more than hunger for adventure; his displaced sexual energy has an esthetic and moral dimension of which he is only dimly aware but which is a major spring of his behavior. He is no longer innocent, but he is still pure. In the life he sees at the training tracks—not, he carefully specifies, at the racing tracks—he senses a natural fraternity: "You hunch down on top of the fence and itch inside of you. Over in the sheds the niggers giggle and sing. Bacon is being fried and coffee made. Everything smells lovely. . . . It just gets you, that's what it does." This is a boy with a vision, and within the limits of what is possible to him it is an admirable vision.

When the boy notices that the trainer of the stallion Sunstreak is as moved as he at watching the horses run, he feels that "there wasn't anything in the world but that man and the horse and me"—a sense of communion that is the essence of the fineness for which he has yearned. But that same night the boy sees the trainer enter a brothel, and through a window watches him staring at a prostitute, "lean and hard-mouthed and . . . a little like the gelding Middlestride." The trainer has the same shine in his eyes as "when he looked at me and at Sunstreak. . . ." And now for the boy "things are different. . . ."

The story revolves around two moments of intense perception, one resulting in joy and the other in pain. The first moment is the boy's sudden awareness that he shares his love for horses with the trainer and the second his shock at discovering the trainer's lust for the prostitute. In this play of symbolic action he learns that the extremes of good and evil can coexist in the same person and can elicit a bewildering similarity of response. Not that the man can love both the pure horse and the contaminated woman, but that he can apparently love both in the same way, is the source of the boy's sorrow. As Cleanth Brooks and Robert Penn Warren have noted, the boy is undergoing an "initiation" into the adult world. Simultaneously, however, the boy, remembering his idealized though nonetheless sexual feeling for horses, fiercely rejects the degraded love between humans he has suddenly witnessed.

The degradation of the brothel is real enough and the boy's revulsion is certainly justified, but the degradation cannot be taken as the only cause of the revulsion. The boy fears the prospect of all adult sexuality, which can never be as "pure" as his relation to horses. So that even as he undergoes his "initiation" into the adult world, he is developing powerful and enduring resistances to it. Life can never again seem so simple and fraternal as it once was; he has entered the blighted arena of knowledge and judgment, he must now confront experience in terms of ambiguity and qualitative distinctions, he must choose rather than absorb. This, then, is Anderson's theme: the niceties of a boy's discriminations and the brutal need to apply them to what he will soon learn to call the real world.

Through the skilled use of a symbolically charged comparison and of a recurrent image, Anderson realizes this theme in dramatic action. The stallion is felt by the boy to be an agent of virility, while the prostitute he instinctively compares to a gelding—which reveals the essence of the story through symbols inherent in the perceptions of its major character. But this meaning is complicated and enriched by a recurrent image of cleanliness through which the boy refers to the sense of purity he had found at the training tracks. For adolescents an obsessive concern with cleanliness indicates a rejection of the "dirty things" grown-ups do. The boy is left with a highly troubled feeling: a realization that he will not be able to satisfy his wish to achieve surface sexual pleasures through his fondness for horses and simultaneously to reject human heterosexuality as unclean and sterile.

In "I Want to Know Why" Anderson completely identifies himself with adolescent feeling: that is, he achieves a triumph of tone. More than most of his stories, which too often tend to a paradigmatic bareness, it deserves Virginia Woolf's praise for creating "a world in which the senses flourish . . . dominated by instincts rather than ideas . . . [in which] race-horses make the hearts of little boys beat high. . . ." In language that reverberates with echoes of the authentic Twain, Anderson does justice to what is distinctly boyish in his boy: "More than a thousand times I've got out of bed before daylight and walked two or three miles to the track." Except for two minor intrusions by an adult voice and several badly superfluous sentences at its end, the story thoroughly maintains the tone and perspective native to its adolescent narrator.

The feeling at the core of "I Want to Know Why" receives several variations, usually more subtle and complex, in the best of Anderson's stories. And in such not wholly successful but still fine pieces as "The Corn Planting," "Brother Death," and "A Meeting South" the possibility of instantaneous and total rapport between two people or between man and nature is again the dominant theme.

"The Corn Planting" is one of Anderson's last stories, subdued and bare. It contains a powerful fable, but lacks sufficient surface representation to transform the fable into a full-bodied story. One evening an old farmer is told by friends that his only son has been killed in the war. Quietly the man returns to his house. A little while later he and his wife are seen walking mutely through their fields in the dead of night, the old man with a hand corn-planter and the old woman with a bag of seed corn. The climax of the story is sufficiently striking as a bit of symbolic grotesquerie to deserve a fuller context:

> They were both in their nightgowns. They would do a row across the field, coming quite close to us as we stood in the shadow of the barn, and then, at the end of each row, they would kneel side by side by the fence and stay silent for a time. The whole thing went on in silence. It was the first time in my life I understood something . . . I mean something about the connection between certain people and the earth—a kind of silent cry, down into the earth, of these two old people, putting corn into the earth. It was as though they were putting death down into the ground that life might grow again. . . .

In "Brother Death" the theme of rapport is presented through an intimate relationship between two children, brother and sister, who make a private circle of their lives because the boy, suffering from heart disease, may die momentarily and the girl alone understands that to confine him is to kill him before death. The figures of Ted and Mary Grey are drawn with lovely tenderness in the story's opening pages, the boy resisting with mute stubbornness all attempts to tame him and the girl, her sensibility inflamed to preternatural proportions, offering him in advance, as it were, what she can of the feminine responses he will never live to enjoy. The girl insists "that

Ted be allowed to die, quickly, suddenly, rather than that death, danger of sudden death, be brought again and again to his attention." And the story boldly hints that in some obscure but essential way the parents are partly the agents of the boy's death: John Grey cuts down two shade trees near his house that have no utility but have given his children much pleasure—an act that is like a killing of luxuriant childhood. The story is muddied by an irrelevant middle, but in its final paragraph returns to the tone of gray somberness Anderson achieves so well:

> But while he lived, there was always, Mary after-wards thought, a curious sense of freedom, something that belonged to him that made it good, a great happiness, to be with him. It was, she finally thought, because having to die his kind of death, he never had to make the surrender his brother had made—to be sure of possessions, success, his time to command—would never have to face the more subtle and terrible death that had come to his older brother.

In "A Meeting South" the theme of rapport receives another variation. The first-person narrator, clearly Anderson himself, introduces David, a young Southern writer apparently modeled after William Faulkner. David has been in the First World War, suffers extreme pain from his wounds, and, as he tries to dull his pain by drinking heavily, has great difficulty in sleeping. The narrator brings David to Aunt Sally, a large old woman who had run a brothel in her youth but now sits at home chatting with young people. Instinctively she senses that David "lived always in the black house of pain. . . ." The narrator feels a throb of satisfaction, he has brought the sensitive young man to a mother. Secure in the unstated affection of the old woman, David tells of his efforts to sleep by drinking whisky to the rhythm of the Negroes who work in the fields by moonlight. In the end, the young writer manages to reach sleep on Aunt Sally's patio. "A Meeting South" occasionally skirts sentimentality and lacks dramatic incident, but if viewed simply as a character sketch it is a fine example of Anderson's gift for gravely lyrical expression.

In three stories, "The Man Who Became a Woman," "The Egg," and "Death in the Woods," Anderson reached the peak of his powers. Judged by no matter how severe standards, these stories are superb bits of fiction, the equal of anything of their kind done in America. Each of them is written in the first person, with the narrator looking back to an adolescent experience, but it would be a sad misreading to think of them only or mainly in terms of adolescence.

The theme of "The Man Who Became a Woman" is much like that of the earlier story, "I Want to Know Why," but to compare the two is to see how the materials of a good story can be reworked into a great one. "The Man Who Became a Woman" is richer in atmospheric texture than the earlier story, it is more certain in technique and consistent in point of view, it benefits greatly from its narrator's distance, and through the most dramatic incident in all of Anderson's fiction it establishes an aura of implicative terror.

Anderson introduces the racetrack milieu with authentic touches possible only to a writer in complete imaginative control of his materials ("when we had got through eating we would go look at our two horses again"). In this atmosphere Herman Dudley meets Tom Means, an educated swipe who, hopes to write stories about horses. "To tell the truth I suppose I got to love Tom . . . although I wouldn't have dared say so, then." Through this sentence both the adolescent actor and the adult he has since become are concretely placed. The adolescent of the past and the adult of the present are not completely separated, as they never can be; and something of the adolescent's love for horses comes through in the adult's remark about Tom Means's effort to "write the way a well bred horse runs"—"I don't think he has," a statement that is less a judgment of Tom Means's literary ability than an offering of loyalty to the narrator's own youth. This narrator is not secure in his male adulthood, for the story he is trying to tell represents a threat he does not quite know how to cope with. At several points he interrupts his narrative to assure the reader, and himself, that the remembered incident was thoroughly unusual in his life. Each return to his narrative then brings another variation on its theme.

He loves Tom Means; he loves horses; he is fond of Negro swipes; and though he begins to dream of women, he is virginal. Precisely his extreme awareness of the affective values available in horses and men prevents him from moving toward full adult sexuality. When he walks his horse after a race, "I wished he was a girl sometimes or that I was a girl and he was a man."

One cold rainy night he is so overcome with loneliness that he wanders into a nearby mining town. In a saloon he sees his face in a mirror: "It was a girl's face . . . a lonesome and scared girl, too." He is afraid that if the men in the saloon see his "girl's face" there will be trouble. But, of course, the men do not notice it, and the only trouble is a brutal brawl that leaves him "sick at the thought of human beings. . . ." Back at the stables, the boy beds down happily in his horse's stall, "running my hands all over his body, just because I loved the feel of him. . . ." But suddenly the stall is invaded by two half-drunk Negroes who mistake him, "my body being pretty white," for a girl. The boy is too terrified to speak—perhaps the Negroes are right. He runs wildly into nearby woods, feeling that "every tree I came close to looked like a man standing there, ready to grab me." The story reaches its grotesque climax when the boy falls across a horse's skeleton near an old slaughterhouse. "And my hands . . . had got hold of the cheeks of that dead horse and the bones of his cheeks were cold as ice with the rain washing over them. White bones wrapped around me and white bones in my hand."

Like "I Want to Know Why," this story is based on a contrast between horses and men, but here the action is less dependent on a naïve moral polarity of animal goodness and human depravity. The horses and men are not, as in the earlier story, independent agents whose moral qualities are measured by an adolescent observer; they are rather mental referents of the moment in adolescence when psychic needs and moral standards clash. That moment is presented with commanding skill: its meaning is extended by a skein of sexual images (horses, faces, dreams, trees) unconsciously employed by the boy, and its alternation between incident and reverie, with reverie mirroring the persistent power of incident in the narrator's mind, results in a tightening clamp of suspense. But the story's greatest power is released when the boy stumbles over the horse's skeleton, a brilliant bit of gothic symbolism. The horse is, of course, a love object of adolescence and, as the boy falls over its skeleton, his hands clutching the bones that are the color of his own girlish skin, he is actually tripping, in terror and flight, over the death of his adolescent love. But his encounter with the skeleton allows of another, yet congruent, reading: by a simple inversion of color, the "white bones wrapped around me and white bones in my hand," as well as the terror felt by the boy when he is enveloped by these bones, may be seen as referring to a forbidden homosexual fantasy. The diffused love of adolescence has been destroyed, but one strand of it survives—and it is this which prompts the narrator to rehearse his experience.

One of the most beautiful qualities of the story is the way in which the adolescent's natural affection for Negroes is seen ripening into the adult's complex social understanding. Herman Dudley awkwardly but movingly explains why Negro swipes, isolated from all social life, might be tempted to molest the sort of white girl found near stables—an explanation completely consistent with the tone of the story. He also blames himself for not having spoken out when the Negroes entered the stall, though he still does not understand why he was unable to; which again indicates that his original confusion about his sexual role persists into his adulthood. And he suggests an additional dimension of ambiguity by remarking that the Negroes were "maybe partly funning." The Negroes thus come to seem subjective shadows of the boy's psychic terror: his experience spins directly from the dislocated center of his self; and the story may be read as if the boy has never actually been molested by the Negro swipes but has erupted into hysteria as a result of accumulated anxieties about his sexual role.

"The Man Who Became a Woman" gains greatly from having an adult narrator who is deeply involved in his own story, for despite his insistence that he is now thoroughly rid of "all that silly nonsense about being a girl" he reveals how persistently, and poignantly, the adult mind struggles to control the memories of adolescence. Herman Dudley may even be, as he insists, a normal man, but to grant this somewhat desperate claim is to record the precariousness and internal ambiguity of adult normality itself. And this, indeed, is the particular achievement of the story, that through a recollection of adolescence it subtly portrays a complex state of adult emotion.

"Death in the Woods" is the only one of Anderson's stories that may accurately be compared, as so many have been, to Russian fiction. Like Turgeniev and Chekhov, Anderson uses the "pathetic fallacy," which is no fallacy at all, to build up the atmosphere of death, and relies on effects of mood and devices of pacing rather than conflict between characters to pull his story into climax. And like Turgeniev and Chekhov in many of their stories, Anderson uses an elemental experience to convey the sense of the ultimate unity of nature, an harmonic oneness of all its parts and creatures bunched in the hand of death.

The story's narrator tells about an old woman, the wife of a lazy and brutal farmer, who has "got the habit of silence." The woman "had to scheme all her life about getting things fed, getting the pigs fed so they would grow fat and could be butchered in the fall." Beaten by her husband and abused by her son, she is the tongueless servant of every living creature near her; "the stock in the barn cried to her hungrily, the dogs followed her about."

On a cold day the old woman wades through snowdrifts to get to town, where she trades her eggs for meat and sugar. With her come four farm dogs, "tall gaunt fellows," who are joined by three other dogs. Carrying a heavy sack of food on her back, she cuts through the woods to reach home before her drunken husband will return from a horse-trading journey. She stops to rest at the foot of a tree, and falls asleep. The day darkens, the moon comes out. The dogs become aroused and begin circling the tree beneath which she sleeps. "Round and round they ran, each dog's nose at the tail of the next dog. In the clearing, under the snow-laden trees and under the wintry moon they made a strange picture, running thus silently, in a circle their running had beaten in the soft snow. The dogs made no sound. They ran round and round in a circle." When the woman dies, the dogs gather round her, do not touch her body but in tearing the food off her back rip her dress. A day or two later the body is found and the boy who is later to remember the incident notices that "She did not look old, lying there in that light, frozen and still. . . . My body trembled with some strange mystical feeling and so did my brother's."

Though bare as a winter tree, the story is marvelously rich in substance. In a note for an anthology Anderson wrote that "the theme of the story is the persistent animal hunger of man. There are these women who spend their whole lives, rather dumbly, feeding this hunger. . . . [The story's aim] is to retain the sense of mystery in life while showing at the same time, at what cost our ordinary animal hungers are sometimes fed." This description is apt, though necessarily limited. For Anderson could hardly have failed to notice that the story may be read as an oblique rendering of what he believed to be the central facts about his mother's life: a silent drudgery in the service of men, an obliteration of self to feed their "persistent animal hunger," and then death.

But "Death in the Woods" obviously strikes much deeper: it is gaunt and elemental, its characters not particularized, the old woman simply a drudge who does not even enjoy the pathetic consolations of Flaubert's Félicité, the husband as brutal as any peasant in Dostoievsky, and the old woman's end as loveless as the most anonymous death. At first the old woman seems an image of the overwhelmed feminine victim, for even the dogs that attend her death are male, but gradually that image is enlarged to include all human creatures; her story becomes the story of all the unnoticed and uninteresting deaths that litter man's time.

While she lives there is nothing beautiful or redeeming about her, but in death she becomes young and radiant in the eyes of the boy, for she is no longer a farmer's wife. Frozen by the nature that is as benevolent to her in death as it was harsh in life, she comes to represent, both to the boy and the men who carry her body back to the town, something far beyond her individual self or possible attributes; something that may be designated as symbolizing the awe felt before fatality. But the particular power of the story is due to the fact that, out of its humility before all sentience, it makes the death of even this most miserable creature seem significant and tragic. In a sense this is the opposite of what Tolstoy did in *The Death of Ivan Ilytch*, yet the two stories have an ironic similarity in that both dramatize the democracy of human fate. The eerie death ceremony performed by the dogs seems as appropriate as any that men could offer, for the old woman's life was no closer to men than to the dogs that circle her in pure hunger, signaling her return to earth. The ceremony of the dogs resolves the story on one level, pointing to the inevitable process of life feeding on fresh death. But simultaneously there is another, more "human" resolution: through observing the woman's death, the boy has enlarged his knowledge of the human condition to which he too is subject; he has learned that an awareness of death is a condition for an intense immersion in life.

"Death in the Woods" has only one significant flaw: a clumsiness in perspective which forces the narrator to offer a weak explanation of how he could have known the precise circumstances of the old woman's death. But in every other respect the story is unblemished: its language, neither colloquial nor literary, is the purest Anderson ever summoned, and its gravely undulating rhythms successfully take its prose to that precarious point which is almost poetry. The story's most brilliant accomplishment in technique is its pacing, its controlled building up and canny holding back, done in the secure knowledge that the climax will not be imperiled by its initial flatness. Anderson reworked "Death in the Woods" several times; and of all his stories he seems to have felt most strongly toward it, for more than any of his autobiographies it expressed his dominant memory of the dark landscape of childhood.

Where "The Man Who Became a Woman" steadily mounts into terror and "Death in the Woods" into awe,

"The Egg" maintains a pace so easy and a tone so mildly wry that, by comparison, it seems almost benign. Yet of Anderson's three best stories it is surely the most terrible in its view of human life, surely the most grim, despairing, and tragic. In the other stories tone seems directly to brace the movement and define the meaning, to provide, as it were, the rising atmospheric tension they require; but in "The Egg" the bare fable is so appalling that, to prevent a slide into the lugubrious, it needs to be cooled by a prose which is dry and unimpassioned. The result, if less conspicuously dramatic than the other stories, is more complex and ironic, and of all Anderson's short fictions "The Egg" most deserves to be placed among the great stories of the world.

The narrator of "The Egg" begins by recalling his parents: his father had been a contented farm hand until, at the age of 35, he married a schoolteacher. Then "they became ambitious. The American passion for getting up in the world took possession of them." To become wealthy they bought a chicken farm, and here the image of the egg, which is to dominate the story with a crazy and malevolent exuberance, first appears. The narrator dryly remembers how difficult it was to raise egg-laying chickens: "It is all so unbelievably complex. . . . One hopes for so much from a chicken and is so dreadfully disillusioned." After ten years of effort the family moves away, to open a restaurant near a railroad junction. But the father takes with him a box full of glass bottles in which malformed baby chicks—four-legged, two-headed, double-winged—are kept in alcohol. By now obsessed with eggs, the father thinks these grotesques valuable, for "people, he said, liked to look at strange and wonderful things." He displays his treasure on a shelf in his restaurant—and the eggs become a curse on the family.

Prodded by an obsession with success, the father conceives the idea of making the restaurant a social center for the neighboring young people. But one night his dream bursts; an egg in hand, he comes upstairs from the store with "a half insane light in his eyes," and falling on his knees begins to weep. The narrator, deliberately avoiding a direct dramatic line, then quietly tells what happened in the store below.

A young man had come in to wait for a train. The father, his eyes lighting on a basket of eggs, began making conversation, insisting that Christopher Columbus was a cheat for falsely claiming to be able to make an egg stand on its head. He, however, could do it, and after many efforts did, but meanwhile the youth, who thought him mildly insane, had failed to notice his feat. Suppressing his anger, the father tried another trick: he heated an egg in vinegar, began to squeeze it through the neck of a bottle and promised that when "the egg is inside the bottle it will resume its normal shape. . . . People will want to know how you got the egg in the bottle. Don't tell them. Keep them guessing." When he heard the approaching train, the father began to hurry. In a panic to please, he broke the egg, splattering it over himself. The indifferent youth laughed, and then "a roar of anger rose from my father's throat. He danced and shouted a string of inarticulate words. Grabbing another egg . . . he threw it, just missing the head of the young man. . . ."

In this story there are two main forces of movement: the father and the egg. It is possible, however, to read it —profitably, if not exhaustively—as though the egg were mere neutral literary furniture and the father the only actor. In such terms, "The Egg" comes to seem, as Horace Gregory has said, "a burlesque of American salesmanship." Here again is the classic American story: ambition prodding a simple man into a situation he cannot control and thereby bringing about his spiritual destruction. And since Anderson felt no need to write from the condescending stance of "social consciousness" he could engage in a fraternal sort of ridicule: "We did not talk much, but in our daily lives tried earnestly to make smiles take the place of glum looks. Mother smiled at the boarders and I, catching the infection, smiled at our cat. Father became a little feverish in his anxiety to please."

When once we take into account the sheer power of the egg to frustrate the father, we must be struck by the extent to which he may be seen as standing for Anderson's own father. Irwin Anderson had a robust heartiness the character in the story does not have, but there were moments in his life when he too collapsed in despair at his own ineptness and the world's unwillingness to take him seriously. From that aspect of his father Anderson has built his character—a poignant gesture of filial reconciliation, sharply in contrast to the murderous aggression of *Windy McPherson's Son* and the self-conscious romanticizing of *A Story Teller's Story*.

But when we extend our focus of perception still further, it becomes clear that the story must finally be read, not primarily as a social portrait or a filial gesture, but as a parable of human defeat. Traditionally, the egg arouses the most intimate associations with the processes of life, but in this story it is to be seen less as a symbol of creativity and renewal than as a token of all the energy in the universe—arbitrary, unmotivated, ridiculous, and malevolent—against which man must pit himself. The image of man suggested by "The Egg" is a deeply pessimistic one: he is not merely defeated but is tricked in his defeat, his very hunger for life is the source of his humiliations, his wish to live becomes his impulsion to death. The world in which he lives is unremittently hostile and, in part, the story's point is to show how the boy gradually realizes the full extent of, and his own subjection to, that hostility. The boy's education in defeat is conveyed through a marvelous symbolic contrast in which the story's tragicomic tone is most sharply realized. He remembers that on Sunday afternoons he used to watch his father sleeping and fancy that the bald path over the top of his head was "a broad road, such a road as Caesar might have made on which to lead his legions" and that he was "going along the road into a far beautiful place where there were no chicken farms and where life was a happy eggless affair." But when, at the moment of his father's humiliation, he sees his mother continually stroking the same bald path, the boy learns where the "broad road" may actually lead to.

As the story proceeds, the egg becomes an increasingly threatening force. It is first seen in its simplest aspect, a commodity to be produced. Then it is a grotesque, the deformation the father values because it is the only kind of egg he can control; an attachment that makes a grotesque out of the father himself. His wish to control the egg and to "entertain" customers are both expressions of a need to enter into workable relations with some force or beings external to himself. But that is beyond his capacity, the egg will be neither toyed with nor controlled, and when, in a revengeful act, he tries to bottle it, the egg breaks over him, causing him his greatest humiliation and driving him still further back into loneliness. In the end, the energy of the egg destroys man.

This is a harsh view, and it is tolerable only because there is nothing harsh in its telling. The egg splatters over the father as the stranger he had sought to please laughs at him—but the boy's mother later runs her hand consolingly over the "bald path." These are the two ultimate images in Anderson's parable of defeat, neither valid without the other, the two together making for the most mature vision of human life Anderson ever had. It is the peculiar virtue of "The Egg" that while each paragraph seems comic its total effect is one of great pathos. And while the story yields a variety of symbolic meanings, it is first and finally a story, thoroughly convincing in the one way a story must be—as a representation of life in which if one wishes, the egg may even be taken as a mere "real" egg.

The number of Anderson's stories that can be considered completely first-rate is few, probably no more than half a dozen, and of these almost all come under the heading of what has here been called his "oral" story form. But those of his stories that are first-rate rank only a shade or two below the best of Chekhov and Turgeniev; their life is assured. It is sometimes argued that they are of limited significance because they are restricted to the subject matter of adolescence; but, as should by now be evident, in Anderson's best stories adolescence becomes a commanding vantage point for imaginative statements about all of human life. In any case, even if the objection were accurate it would be of little significance, for only the genuinely mature artist can portray immature life. Anderson's "oral" stories, it is true, do not create the large social world that is often demanded of fiction, and they hardly create the kind of world, as does *Winesburg*, that is primarily the outer sign of a subjective vision. But this much they do: they impinge irrevocably on the reader's sensibility, enlarging his knowledge of and insight into men—and that is the ultimate test of fiction.

Anderson's remaining stories are, by and large, not so successful as those based on the pattern of oral narrative. When his stories are patently "written," when they do not depend on a central narrator for their movement and meaning, they lack the tonal unity and structural tidiness of the "oral" stories. (The distinction between Anderson's "oral" and "written" stories is not quite the same as that between his stories in the first and third person, for there are several in the third person, such as "Brother Death" and "An Ohio Pagan," in which one clearly feels the presence of a narrator's voice.) A few of the stories that do not follow the oral pattern are, of course, successful, notably "The Untold Lie" and "The Return," an effective account of a man's disappointing visit to his home town. But in most of the "written" ones there is no sufficiently realized dramatic action or engaging character to replace the oral narrator as a centripetal force. The stories consequently tend to thin into musings or symbolic schemes.

Thematically, this second group of stories is usually concerned with the neurotic costs of the unlived life. In such stories as "Unlighted Lamps" and "The Door of the Trap" people are locked in their inability to communicate, and experience evades them while they hunger for it. Mary Cochran, who appears in both stories, bears the curse of her father's original failure to warm his marriage with the emotion that "was straining and straining trying to tear itself loose." The theme of unlived life receives two major variations, first as a fear of expressing emotion ("Unlighted Lamps") and then as a hesitation to accept sex from which love might follow ("The Door of the Trap"). What the source of this appalling isolation is, Anderson does not feel a need to say; sometimes he hints that it is a heritage of Puritanism or of Midwestern town harshness, but it seems clear that in his deepest feelings he regards isolation as an ineradicable human condition.

Both variations of the theme of unlived life appear in "Out of Nowhere, Into Nothing," a long story that is probably his most characteristic expression. Rosalind Westcott returns to her native Iowa town for a brief visit, hoping to talk to her mother and to weigh her life in Chicago, but as she observes the kindly sloth in which her parents live and hears again those terrible "night noises" she had hated as a girl, she realizes that her family cannot help her; she is alone. Like many of Anderson's women, Rosalind Westcott is strong and vital, full of desire for an experience that can engage her emotional capacities. While walking along a railroad track in the corn fields, she meets her next-door neighbor, Melville Stoner, a bachelor who assumes the stance of the reflective observer. She is drawn to him, to his queerness and his trembling wish for companionship. For a moment it seems as if she has found with him "the thing beyond words, beyond passion—the fellowship in living," but

Melville Stoner withdraws, pleading that he is too old to abandon his passive role.

Midway, Anderson resorts to long murky flashbacks to Rosalind's Chicago years, and the story slumps badly. But as long as he focuses on Rosalind Westcott and Melville Stoner, who are among his more individualized and memorable characters, the story has a gray, resigned poignancy: the image of these two lonely people walking in the yellow heat of the Iowa corn fields remains fixed in one's mind. The story's greatest strength is as a portrait of male inadequacy, of a good man's refusal to enter the dangerous relationships of love and sex. A woman's desire and a man's loneliness meet, there is a brief parabola of intense feeling and then: parting, each unable to satisfy the other. Of Melville Stoner, Anderson asks, "Did loneliness drive him to the door of insanity, and did he also run through the night seeking some lost, some hidden and half-forgotten loveliness?" Here in one sentence are gathered Anderson's most characteristic and cherished words: *door, run, hidden, half-forgotten, loveliness;* here is his world. The view behind "Out of Nowhere, Into Nothing" is untenable in itself: to believe life to be a mere occasional explosion in the darkness and to insist so literally on human isolation is a kind of perverse romanticism. But when enough feeling enters into Anderson's fictional rendering of this view, it becomes enlarged and complicated in a way its abstract statement never can be—which is a measure of the artist's triumph.

In most of the stories that deal with the theme of unlived life there is, however, as great an emotional deprivation in their own telling as their characters are supposed to suffer; Anderson allows his dominating notion to weed promiscuously and to choke off the dramatic representation necessary to fiction. When one examines such stories as "Another Man's Wife," "The Man's Story," "Unused," "The Door of the Trap," and "The New Englander," one is struck by how remarkably devoid they are of any account of external experience, how vague in background and hazy in evocation of place and thing. The typical Anderson characters are here all so very familiar: all straining, bursting into nothingness, all lost. Though Anderson's intention is a call to experience, these stories are often evasions of the writer's obligation to focus on particular segments of experience; they create an unprovisioned and unlimned world, a neither-nor area suspended between reality and symbol. Toward his undifferentiated gargoyles Anderson feels and shows the tenderest of loves, but his absorption in a world that is neither descriptively faithful nor symbolically coherent can lead to nothing but a declining sputter of emotion at the end of each story. Having abandoned or rather having never fully accepted realism, he could not find, in these stories, another method for perceiving the objective world. He was trapped in a halfway house: he could neither build realistic structures nor find an adequate means of transcending the need for them.

In this second group of his stories he would often employ elaborate systems of symbolism to sustain his story where neither his action nor his characters could. In "The New Englander," for example, there is an extraordinary skein of symbols but the story itself lacks the conviction of reality; there is nothing viable in relation to which the symbols can act. Anderson is not presenting genuinely conceived characters, he is redecorating the legend of

Puritan repression through such symbols as the rock, the trapped rabbit, the imprisoned bird. Here symbols do not enlarge upon reality; they crush it.

Another frequent sign of disintegration in these stories is Anderson's resort to rigid verbal rhythms which he apparently hoped would serve as the controlling and soothing center of his prose. In those pieces where he is most at sea imaginatively, the rhythm is most insistently established, as for example in the story "Unused":

> How cruelly the town had patronized May, setting her apart from the others, calling her smart. They had cared about her because of her smartness. She was smart. Her mind was quick, it reached out.

Here the deliberate reiteration of one simple word makes for an increasingly stiff cadence and an irritatingly false simplicity. When Anderson has his writing under control the rhythm is subterranean and bracing; as soon as the relationship between medium and meaning is disturbed, the rhythmic beat becomes a grating staccato responsible for that air of disingenuous folksiness which disfigures so much of his writing.

In Anderson's stories it is thus possible to see most clearly that major contrast in quality which is present in all of his work. The first group of stories, together with *Winesburg*, is his most valuable achievement, unquestionably an enrichment of the American imagination; the second group is not merely bad in itself but soon comes to seem a portent of the particular kind of badness which is to pervade both Anderson's later novels and much of American fiction in the twentieth century.

In the Lawrencian Orbit

DURING his summer vacation in 1916 Sherwood Anderson was exposed to a major cultural shock; he heard Trigant Burrow, one of the first American psychoanalysts, discuss those portions of Freudianism which had reached America. Anderson had previously listened to vague talk about Freud's theory of dreams, but as a literary apprentice calculatingly shy of systematic thought and completely absorbed in his own work, he had been unable to understand its full importance. Now, however, as Burrow talked to him during long walks in the woods near Lake Chateaugay, Anderson reacted quickly and excitedly. Two years later he wrote to Burrow that "much of what you told me that summer . . . I have found to be true."

That truth did not reach him without first meeting the usual resistance. In "Seeds," a fictional record of his conversations with Burrow, Anderson remembered himself as saying: "It is given to no man to venture far along the road of lives. . . . The illness you pretend to cure is the universal illness. The thing you want to do cannot be done . . . do you expect love to be understood?" Burrow replied that the "universal illness" might at least be alleviated—though years later he was to feel that Anderson's doubts about individual therapy had constituted a brilliant intuition. Anderson himself, like most American writers, gradually learned to respect the power of the Freudian system, which he was always to see less as a set of therapeutic recommendations than a powerful sanction for the struggle against Puritan repression and a group of insights into the economy of the unconscious.

As his work became known in the 1920's Anderson was quickly tagged a Freudian, usually by critics who assumed a causal connection between Freud's theories and the portraiture of neurotic character-types in *Winesburg*. He was often labeled the American writer most influenced by Freud, and in *The Dial* Miss Alyse Gregory had a myopic vision of Anderson "like the anxious white rabbit in Alice in Wonderland clasping . . . the latest edition of Sigmund Freud." Regis Michaud, an extravagant Freudian critic, hailed him as "the Freudian novelist *par excellence*" and Camille McCole, a Catholic critic, denounced him in much the same terms. The critics were going largely by several references in *Poor White* to what could be read as psychoanalytical concepts, and the remark in *Dark Laughter* that "if there is anything you do not understand in human life, consult the works of Doctor Freud." To his friends Anderson kept insisting, however, that he had not read Freud, and in his *Memoirs* he was to add "I never did read him."

This statement, no matter how many of Anderson's friends testify to its accuracy, it is impossible to believe. That the internal evidence from his books means little is true: he could have gleaned the stock Freudian phrases from the literary environment. But can one really believe that during the two decades he heard himself linked to the famous "Doctor Freud" Anderson never tried to read his books? Is this not at variance with everything we know about human vanity and curiosity, qualities in which Anderson was happily not deficient? Far more credible is the assumption that, despite what he told his friends, he did try to read Freud and found him too difficult or too scientific.

Toward Freud Anderson could feel little warmth: he seemed too austere, too systematic. Most of what interested him in Freud's ideas and little of what seemed forbidding in Freud, he found in D. H. Lawrence—a vision of a more passionate life, a morality by which to affirm the body, and a *Weltanschauung* which could shatter social conventions. It was with Lawrence, not with Freud, that he had a close imaginative affinity; but before Lawrence could break through to him, Freud had to establish an entirely new intellectual climate.

Anderson first read Lawrence at Paul Rosenfeld's suggestion. In January 1921 he was sending Rosenfeld some shrewd comments on *Women in Love*: "I feel that so sophisticated a manner is in some way indicative of spiritual uneasiness. . . . It is a terrific struggle he has gone through. What courage and fortitude he has shown." A week later his doubts were gone: "Have just finished Lawrence's book. It's tremendous . . . like a storm I once lived through . . . Lawrence went after something —a feeling that in some queer way rides over all thought and he came very near pulling it off. . . ."

With no other contemporary writer could Anderson identify himself so closely as with Lawrence. Joyce he admired from a distance (when they met in 1927 they had little to say to each other), but Lawrence he freely acknowledged as his literary master, difficult though that acknowledgment must have been. How painful it could actually become Anderson learned shortly after the publication of *Lady Chatterley's Lover*. When his friends, James Fiebleman and Julius Friend, gave him a copy of Lawrence's novel, he read through it quickly and then rushed to them in a mood both rapturous and despairing: this, he told them, was the great novel of modern love, the novel he had hoped to write but which, having been "dispossessed" of the subject by Lawrence, he would now never write. The notion of "dispossessing" need not be taken seriously for one to see in Anderson's reaction the poignancy of a minor artist overwhelmed and humbled by the achievement of a major one. For the rest of his life Anderson continued to have this special feeling for Lawrence, a blend of pain and joy, and when Lawrence died he wrote a tribute to "a kingly man." Just short of accurate and yet imaginatively right, Anderson's description of Lawrence was a rare gesture of literary chivalry, all the finer in that it came from a man increasingly aware of how seldom he could summon "kingliness" in his own life or work.

In *Many Marriages*, the first of Anderson's novels to deal entirely with modern sexual experience, the influence of Lawrence is already present, though less in theme and situation than in Anderson's wish to inspire it with "a complete and absolute acceptance of flesh." Far more than flesh, however, the book "accepts" as its emotional premise a pervasive American daydream, a fantasy in which the businessman sees himself painlessly escaping his adult ties. *Many Marriages* contains neither the elaborately structured and censored apprehensions of waking life nor the rich confusion of images found in night-dreams; its materials are rather the naïve wilfulness and delicious self-acclaim of the daydream. Partly a rehearsal of Anderson's private legend, it is also a close reflection of a public experience which American folklore acknowledges to be peculiarly our own.

One spring John Webster, a middle-aged manufacturer, is sexually aroused by his secretary, Natalie Swartz, whom he values mainly for her clear complexion and laconic availability. No longer able to tolerate his lumpish asexual wife and repressed daughter, Webster begins to lock himself in his room, where he parades in the nude and ruminates before a portrait of the Virgin. During one of these private rites he calls in wife and daughter to announce that he is leaving them; the wife collapses, but the daughter, stirred by Webster's ambiguous caresses, listens eagerly to his account of why his marriage failed. As Webster runs off with Natalie, he is convinced that he has saved his daughter from frigidity, though toward his wife, who commits suicide, he feels "no sense of guilt." Wondering whether he really loves Natalie or is merely using her to justify his flight, he soon consoles himself with the reflection that if "he and Natalie . . . could not live together, there was still life."

There was still life!—for Anderson the novelist always in the future, never immediately apprehended in its complexity or richness or sheer novelty. As Edmund Wilson noted in *The Dial* shortly after the book appeared: "Mr. Anderson's habit of stripping his characters of their incidentals—their clothes, their furniture and their social relations—which in his best stories produces a classic simplicity, in *Many Marriages* leaves them strangely pale, as if they had been stripped of their personalities, too." Though mildly put, Wilson's remark was actually the harshest thing that could be said about a novel. When a novelist does not care for the uniqueness of his characters he substitutes notions about them for representation of them; which is equivalent to a betrayal of his craft. And *Many Marriages* is notion-ridden, each notion so blithely advanced by Anderson that he can ignore with light conscience the undisposed problems of his story.

The result is a cruel parody of his intention. A novel meant to celebrate sex fails completely to show sexual desire or the sexual relation. Toward his wife Webster can feel only a numb sadism, toward his daughter a thinly disguised incestuous yearning, and toward the inarticulate Natalie an impersonal, almost absent-minded desire which in their one physical meeting quickly regresses to a variety of infantile groping. Sex is talked about, buzzed about—but is not there. What is there is an arbitrary redressing of reality to salve a bruised male will. Never does Webster ask himself whether he might bear some responsibility for his wife's frigidity; never does Anderson, a novelist committed to "life," ask the question for him. Nor does Anderson think to inquire why Webster's affair should be expected to end any better than his marriage. Anderson's view of love seems here to be something like the game of musical chairs: what matters is that one keep moving.

So thoroughly does Anderson approve of Webster that he allows no character to assume a critical relation toward his mind. And the quality of Webster's mind is revealed in a speech he directs to the portrait of the Virgin: "I hope you are a true virgin. . . . I brought you into this room and into the presence of my nude body because I thought you would be that. You see, being a virgin you cannot have anything but pure thoughts." In intention Webster is the liberated sexual hero; in effect a fatuous buffoon.

The theme of *Many Marriages* can still be defended as "in itself" valid; in American life repression inflicts a fearful damage, and to escape it is both right and necessary. But it is the perverse badness of the novel that it soon reduces its own truth to a half-truth—which is to say, finally to an untruth; and that this reduction is the consequence not of a corrupt intention but of an indifference to those pressures of complexity which must beset every truth and without which no truth can long survive.

In *Many Marriages* the hunger for experience has become an obsession blinding Anderson to anything that might resemble heterogeneous experience. That obsession is also loose in *Dark Laughter*, but this latter novel is less insulated by raw conviction and is therefore occasionally open to a rush of reality. In one sense, it can be read as a reaction against the earlier book: Bruce Dudley, its central figure, has attained the urban bohemianism for which a John Webster yearns, but he finds that living in a "studio apartment" with a wife who writes newspaper fiction and cooks badly leaves him chronically discontented. Anderson is surprisingly eloquent about the dreary tastelessness of the "modern" semi-intellectual and the sado-masochistic debasements of his love-life: the superfluous husband and the career-busy wife now think of each other as competitors rather than mates and burn with the wish to inflict or receive violence.

If the life of realization is not to be found in Bohemia, then perhaps, suggests Anderson, it may be found by a return to those areas that sophistication has not yet corrupted and left impotent. Bruce Dudley leaves his wife, visits New Orleans where he is entranced by the sensual laughter of the Negroes, settles to an anonymous life as a small-town factory hand, attracts the restless eye of Aline Grey, his employer's wife, and takes a job as her gardener. Though not exactly a Mellors (the anticipation is largely occupational), Dudley persuades her to leave with him for that hazy vista of freedom which had so unsettled John Webster. Meanwhile there rings a chorus of mocking laughter from the Greys' Negro servants, to whom the neurotic antics of the whites seem marvelously ridiculous.

In several bits of the book Anderson begins to grasp what the novelist's business should be. Dudley's married life is sketched with bitter intensity; Aline's bourgeois husband is vividly caricatured; Dudley and Grey compete in a harshly humorous foot-race, each pretending to ignore the other but both feeling that a test of virility is somehow involved. And in a romantic but controlled portrait of Sponge Martin, an old craftsman who likes to recall his days as a carriage painter, Anderson achieves his authentic tone.

But, like its predecessor, *Dark Laughter* is cruelly marred by Anderson's unwillingness—unwillingness at least as much as inability—to qualify his motivating notion with sufficiently fine observation and knowledge. The call to erotic fulfillment, even if reduced to primitivism, is never one to be slighted, but erotic fulfillment can hardly be achieved through mere sincerity, certainly not through the fumbling spiritless sincerity which is Dudley's emotional capital. (This strain of ineffectuality in a novel dedicated to the vital life may be one reason for its popular appeal in the 1920's: it seemed to offer Lawrence's vision without the accompanying pain, effort, and hysteria. Unfortunately once the pain, effort, and hysteria were discarded, the vision had maliciously shrunk to mere platitude.)

In the novels he composed under Lawrence's influence Anderson was unable to treat ideas with dialectical fluidity, to see them in potential change and place them in tense relations to hostile ideas; he merely affirmed that with which he had begun, the life of realization. This is why his call to primitive wholeness could slip into an attitude toward women that is mere reactionary bovinism ("They were onto women, the French. The idea was to . . . use them, make them serve"); or into a coarse antiintellectualism; or into oversimplified and patronizing notions about Negroes ("Negro women have no moral sense. They will do anything. They like it. . . .") There might be some point in a novelist's contrasting the impotence of white society with the presumably healthier sex life of the Negroes, but only if he were willing to use his eyes and his mind to the extent of noticing that Negroes can hardly be immune to the neuroses that besiege the whites.

Anderson's treatment of Jewish character in *Dark Laughter* also raises some problems. When Fred Grey remembers a Jew he met during the war, "a large man with curly hair and a big nose," and reflects that it was odd to see "a Jew fighting for his country," it is possible and even plausible to credit Anderson with not sharing Grey's feeling, for Grey is not a favorable character. But one is disturbed when Bruce Dudley, the sympathetic hero of the novel with whom Anderson clearly identifies himself, wonders: "Could he ever really know a Jew, a German, a Frenchman, an Englishman?"—as if a Jew were an unmet and inaccessible foreigner. There is further cause for disturbance when Dudley is sharply juxtaposed to a "flashy young Jew" who writes clever copy in Dudley's newspaper office and represents the facile commercialism he would escape. It is easy enough to imagine the existence of such a "word-slinger," but one wonders what relevance his Jewishness (he is not otherwise identified) has to the corruption of his talent, an unfortunate waste hardly unique to Jews.

No problem of bias is involved in Anderson's description of Jewish characters. If one cared to draw up a balance sheet, it would be possible to find favorable passages about the Jews to match the disturbing passages. (One Jewish character is a soldier who in a difficult situation rises to a humane response.) What Anderson's treatment of Jews in this novel seems to indicate is that, in addition to the spontaneous affection and tolerance he displayed throughout his life, there remained in him a preconscious remnant of that folk stereotype which regards Jews as the archetypal "other," alien, unknowable, and perhaps suspect. This stereotype is also present in the work of such other American novelists as Wolfe and Fitzgerald.

It is interesting that the Jewish characters in *Dark Laughter* are all nameless. There are other unnamed characters in Anderson's books, but they are usually identified by some trait of individual idiosyncrasy or by their occupation or by their distinctive physical appearance; they are not summarily labeled Catholic or Protestant. The Jewish characters, however, are located in terms of their presumed group cohesion—as if that were a sufficient means to specify character. While one is certain that Anderson intended neither hostility nor malice, his resort to an unexamined folk stereotype in portraying Jews seems another instance of that thoughtlessness which afflicts the entire book.

To speak now of these two novels in relation to the works that most influenced their composition, D. H. Lawrence's *The Rainbow* and *Women in Love,* may seem almost like a bad joke, a beating of failure with the nailed stick of genius. But it is a comparison which Anderson in his more courageous moments would have accepted, even if with the foreknowledge that it could bring him little joy; a comparison valuable not only as a measure of achievement but for what it may reveal about Anderson's failure to assimilate the Lawrencian theme.

Of Lawrence's novels after *Sons and Lovers* it is often said that they are hardly novels at all. In support of this view Lawrence's famous letter is repeatedly quoted in which he declared himself bored with the conventional novel form and intent on abandoning "that hard violent style full of sensation and presentation." While transforming himself from a novelist into a prophet, Lawrence is thereupon supposed to have ceased creating characters and to have rendered only states of consciousness.

There is but one convenient way of characterizing this view: it is wrong. That Lawrence was partly responsible for it does not lessen its wrongness. The general distinction between the creating of character and the rendering of states of consciousness is not likely to bear close investigation, and with regard to Lawrence's novels themselves is, moreover, largely inaccurate. Anna Brangwen is as thoroughly realized a character as any in English fiction, and Rupert Birkin is more visualized physically, more immediate sensually, more scoured emotionally and intellectually than most males in the English novel. It is true that there is a change in Lawrence's method from *Sons and Lovers* to *The Rainbow* and that in addition to depicting characters in external action he now tries to pierce, as it were, to the centers of their being. It is also true that by *The Rainbow* he has begun to write in a prophetic manner. But his writing is nonetheless still "full of sensation and presentation," and the prophet in him is seldom the man who makes statements, in or out of novels, *about* things—seldom indeed when he talks about the "religion of blood," or plays the social bully, or becomes infatuated with his presumptive godliness, or sounds off with fascist and anti-Semitic remarks. He is a prophet only when he is a great novelist; his prophecy is his presentation, his presentation his prophecy.

Part of this prophecy consists in the rarest truth-telling about modern love, his knowledge of the love-struggle between Anna and Will Brangwen, his insight into the impotence of Hermione Roddice, and his manly willingness to grant that some of that impotence has crippled even Birkin, which is to say, himself. He offers no program: he is honest enough never to suggest anything more than a bitter and painful struggle for sexual health. But he does offer something more valuable than a program: an occasional vision of the sexual meeting in its full and liberating power. He cannot present a sustained view of a life ordered by sexual-emotional health; only flashes: Anna and Will Brangwen burning out their aggressions and then meeting fiercely, Birkin and Ursula Brangwen coming together in a rare ecstasy. But these flashes are precisely the margin of genius in Lawrence's work; nothing like them had ever before appeared in English fiction; sex had indeed been adumbrated but never presented in its full tension, purity, and ultimate "otherness." And since the flashes were new Lawrence had to improvise, as he remarked, "another language almost."

This is Lawrence's unique achievement, an achievement in which the novelist and the prophet are inseparable; it is what Anderson hoped for but could not summon.

Why he could not do what Lawrence did—can this question be answered? We simply do not know why one man is endowed with genius and another not, and when we try to explain genius we usually do little more than itemize the very qualities which originally prompted us to speak of it. But even if our answer is no more than a discrete breaking-down of the question, it may help explain Anderson's failure when writing about modern life.

Once the comparison between Lawrence and Anderson is pushed beyond the simple fact of influence, it becomes clear that for all the similarities in their versions of life, they were, in themselves and in relation to the world, vastly different men. While still young Lawrence had already finished with most of the preliminaries of life: he knew, for good or ill, exactly the terms on which he meant to live. His practice may never have equaled his conception—which is proof of what need not be proved, his fallible humanity; but to be committed to a conception so rigorous as his was itself no small practice. Ander-

son, however, could never quite finish with the preliminaries of life for he had never had enough of them: he
was forever intent on making up for lost time, forever
subject to an insatiable hunger for experience abstract and
ultimate, forever ready to inundate himself in each wave
of cultural fashion which upon receding left him sick and
floundering. Lawrence had a commanding grasp of Western culture when he decided it was not enough, Anderson
had only scraps and fragments. Lawrence acted from the
strength of secure renunciation, Anderson from the weakness of enforced deprivation.

A vision so radical as the rediscovery of man's physical
core and therewith his psychic health could be sustained
only by a writer who had achieved a rich and pressing relation, albeit an antagonistic one, to the highest kinds of
civilized accomplishment. Lawrence had thoroughly ex-
plored and completely *knew* what he was rejecting; Anderson's rejection, one must often suspect, was part of
his failure to know. In Lawrence the vision of sexual re-
generation could accordingly come through in occasional
completeness, while in Anderson it was almost always
muddied by his characteristically American concern with
liberating himself from one or another clamp of a provincial society. His work was forever stained by the values
of the "Chicago Renaissance," that attempt to surmount
with rawness a raw society; and it is these values which so
often make his call to erotic fulfillment seem egotistical,
frivolous, simplistic. A writer still tied to a repressive environment can only rarely create a satisfactory vision of
freedom, for he has first to liberate himself and, more
often than not, in the painful process of liberation he will
exhaust and destroy himself. But Lawrence had already

gone beyond this; he was no longer a mere victim, he could assume an active relation to society despite his mourning over "the absolute frustration of my primeval societal instinct." In his *Studies in Classic American Literature* Lawrence noticed the pervasive American yearning to "get away," and it was this yearning which Anderson confused, could not but confuse, with his vision of sexual primacy. The consequence of such a confusion Lawrence had foreseen: "Which is all very well, but it isn't freedom. Rather the reverse. A hopeless sort of constraint. It is never freedom till you find something you really *positively want to be.*"

In Anderson the call to primitivism was tinged with a feckless irresponsibility, hardly a quality sufficient for a prophetic reconstruction of human life. In Lawrence the call to primitivism was largely a parable of a psychic journey modern man had to take. Lawrence railed against "mental consciousness," the brittle rationalism and febrile intellectuality of his friends, but he possessed and proudly cultivated an extremely powerful mind. Anderson, however, took too literally—which is to say, with insufficient seriousness—the Lawrencian notion that to reassert the glory of the body man would have to depreciate the value of the mind. It is only necessary to compare Lawrence's letters with those of Anderson to see the difference between a mind of catholic range and penetration and a mind too often content with its own confusions. Lawrence could sometimes reach the depths of human feeling because his mind was so restless, so curious, so unceasingly active; Anderson was trapped by his sterile notions because his mind was too unused, too deliberately and programmatically unused. What is *Many Marriages* but a stubborn and, as it were, principled refusal to think? And what is the price of that refusal if not a numb inability to feel?

We must escape, we must celebrate incessantly our burst into the light and never inquire what our behavior is to be once we arrive in the light—this was the compulsive notion behind Anderson's writing about modern life; and, like all notions that neither rise to the power of thought nor sink to the power of emotion, it crippled his work. He believed in sex: but where in his work was the struggle between lovers that Lawrence so marvelously showed in *The Rainbow?* where was the patient representation of the social context in which man is to revitalize his sexual life? where was the knowledge of its relation to money, ambition, politics? and where, above all, was sexuality itself? Anderson could see sex only in one of its possible outer relations: he sensed that between personal impotence and the automatism of the factory there was a certain connection. But except for this one valuable insight, sex in Anderson's novels was little more than a compulsive gesture which ironically recalled the fable of failure he had composed in "The Egg." There was, indeed, a certain tenderness in these novels, not the glowing tenderness of *Winesburg* or of "Death in the Woods"—fictions in which Anderson had found an object, a social memory through which to realize himself—but a tenderness of unacknowledged defeat and sometimes of willed evasion. By contrast Lawrence had something of the bully in him—it was one of his least attractive traits; but it was there because he struggled so desperately to achieve secure manhood. In *Many Marriages* and *Dark Laughter*, however, Anderson's tenderness signified that the fulfillment for which his characters yearned was never quite to be attained.

It is startling to see how often Anderson's novels are dominated by a fear of sex or at least a highly disturbed feeling toward it. In *Windy McPherson's Son* Sam Mc-Pherson's marriage night is sexless and "pure," and his wife is later unable to give birth to the children she carries. In *Marching Men* Beaut McGregor is a grumpy misogynist. In *Poor White* Hugh McVey runs away from his bride on their wedding night and not till four years later do they have normal relations. In *Many Marriages* the frigidity of John Webster's wife would be seen as a reflection on Webster's sexual condition by any novelist who took the trouble to think. And in *Dark Laughter* Bruce Dudley remembers "times, two or three of them, when he had been with women and had been ineffectual. Perhaps he had been ineffectual with Bernice. Had he been ineffectual or had she?"

Such a persistence of theme can hardly be accidental, and though one must be extremely cautious in taking imaginative works as evidence about an author's life, it seems reasonably clear that for the man who wrote these novels sex was a source of deep anxiety. Of course, sexual difficulty can be as valid a fictional theme as sexual realization—but only when recognized for what it actually is. In such novels as *Many Marriages* and *Dark Laughter* there is, however, a ghastly split between intention and achievement: Anderson believes he is showing a movement to health when in actuality his characters are as sick at the end of the books as at the beginning. Not sex but sexual anxiety dominates these novels, and the fact that they could once be taken as "sex-centered" shows how tenuous and sickly the American sense of sex actually is.

Lawrence too had his moments of intense anxiety, as his portrait of Rupert Birkin makes clear. But unlike Anderson he possessed a thorough awareness of his own situation, an unhesitating readiness to face it both in his life and his work, and the courage not to confuse the reality with his wishes. He was consequently able to conduct a relatively successful struggle for the conditions of life that would allow his energies to flow easily and richly into both his work and his relations with people. In effect: Lawrence had Frieda, and Anderson several wives.

The pervasive image of impotence, accompanied by a low-charged tone that itself seems impotent before the multiplicity of life, is the final impression left by those of Anderson's novels written in the Lawrencian orbit. His intention was to depict sexual struggle, sexual relations, sexual feeling; the actuality he had himself unwittingly described years back when he wrote of Windy McPherson's public failure: "the thing, he felt, was in him, and it was only a fatal blunder in nature" that it did not come through triumphantly.

The Downward Curve

TO A public stenographer who copied one of his stories in 1925, Sherwood Anderson seemed most memorable for his "leisurely, reassuring calmness," his air of "large-hearted tolerance." Casual though this impression was, it accurately took in a significant side of Anderson's public personality: the Anderson who wore loose tweeds and blithely announced that the prose rhythms of *Dark Laughter* derived from *Ulysses*, who told a friend he at last felt himself on the verge of sophistication and exchanged letters with Alfred Stieglitz about the artist's struggle to survive in a hostile society. That he had achieved fame caused him to feel both awe and amusement, but the fame was nonetheless there, to be enjoyed or exploited or, most pleasurable of all, brushed carefully aside. From people throughout the country he received letters confessing the secrets of their hearts and thanking him for having expressed the gnarled aspirations of American life. And whatever else might happen to him, he was secure in the knowledge that he was the author of *Winesburg, Ohio*, a book he would soon be referring to as an American classic—which might have been offensive had it not been so incontestably true. In twelve years he had transformed his life as few Americans before or since, and if he now seemed assured and calm, if he radiated tolerance and kindliness, only the most ungenerous could have challenged his right to those feelings.

Four years later Anderson was to be as lost in despair as a man can be this side of suicide. In retrospect it seems clear that the personal and creative disintegration which was to reach a climax in 1929 had already begun at about the time of his third marriage and had become quite noticeable during the public success of *Dark Laughter*. Yet the impression of the stenographer who saw in Anderson only self-assurance was accurate too, and at the moment most perceptibly so. Anderson was not the least complex of men, and even as the curve of his public success rose, another and more intimate curve began to slope toward crisis. He was to resist this inner disintegration and, in some ways, to resist it successfully; but in the years between 1925 and the outbreak of the Depression his struggle with and within himself was continuous and its outcome never certain.

What worried him most was his future as a writer. There remain from this period a good many unpublished manuscripts in which repeated efforts to break through to a new subject matter betray both creative uncertainty and a growing awareness of that uncertainty. Anderson was now in the painful position of a writer to whom subject matter, no longer welling up as irresistible necessity, has become a conscious "problem." He felt that he had exhausted the theme and setting of *Winesburg*, he was increasingly doubtful about his novels (in the future, he told Paul Rosenfeld, Anderson the writer would "wear clothes"), and he had not accumulated a sufficient reserve of observations about modern life from which a subject matter might organically arise. To Rosenfeld he wrote: "I have come to care only for working people, negroes and very fine sophisticated people. . . . Shall I be forced to become the voice of laborers, negroes etc.?" These uneasy remarks, close to being false of tone, come from a writer floundering midway in his career, a writer weary of boyhood memories yet involved only in haphazard and therefore precarious relations to adult experience.

One symptom of anxiety, almost inevitable among writers, was his increasing worry about money. The worry itself was an old one (in 1919 he had asked Trigant Burrow to find an "angel" willing to give him $2500 a year!) and it was certainly justified now. But the nagging persistence of this worry leads one to suspect that it must have had a significance beyond the terms in which it was conceived. It can hardly be an accident that references in his letters to money troubles often go together with explicit remarks and unwitting hints about a crisis in his creative life.

During these years the idea of an "angel" kept buzzing through Anderson's head, his conviction that as an artist he deserved one being bolstered by his hope, probably a remnant of his old salesman psychology, that he could find one. The odd thing is that he did so—not, to be sure, until 1927 but still in time to ease the last years of his life. Burton Emmett, a wealthy advertising man with a fabulous passion for every scrap of paper on which Anderson ever scribbled, became his patron in 1927 and extended him a rare generosity; after Emmett's death in the mid-1930's his wife continued to help Anderson.

Meanwhile other props had to be found, and in early 1925 Anderson took to the lecture platform. Though profitable, lecturing was loathsome to him, and it seems to have drained his energy more than that of most writers. He was a poor speaker, given, between glimpses at his prepared manuscript, to nervous pacing across the platform. Lecturing to women's clubs seemed to him not only an indignity but also an exposure to the taunts of the very philistines he had attacked in his books. To Gertrude Stein he wrote in the spring of 1925: "Made a little money and often an ass of myself. . . . They fear I will piss against the leg of the man who is introducing me or bring on the stage a lady and do her violence there to promote higher life. . . ." This not unpleasing vision of himself was, unfortunately, hardly warranted by his experience as a lecturer, for his audiences usually accorded him a considerable if uncomprehending respect. The lectures themselves were rather vapid: one of them, "The Modern Writer," began well enough with a description of the American artist's problems which reads like a plebeian restatement of Henry James's famous remarks in his study of Hawthorne, but it soon lapsed into the trite phrases about Puritanism and Commercialism that were Anderson's Chicago legacy; another, "America, A Storehouse of Vitality," was a call to resistance against modern mechanization, very probably influenced by the blazing letters he had been getting from Alfred Stieglitz on that theme. At the end of 1925, when Anderson had completed a long lecture trip, he wrote to his agent, Otto Liveright: "I shall not do it again unless I am badly broke." What Anderson needed now was to re-examine his life and confront himself as an artist; instead, his lecturing brought only weariness, dispersion of creative energy, and distraction of mind. By keeping him "busy" his lecture trips postponed the moment when he would have to ask himself: what shall I do now? That moment, however, came soon enough, and when it did it stretched out over several years.

By mid-1925 at least Anderson's financial problems seemed happily solved. Horace Liveright, a speculator with a taste for letters whom Anderson remembered as "rather crazy, rather splendid," was then collecting the best American writers by the simple but unassailable method of offering them more generous terms than other publishers. A five-year contract providing for $100 a week as advance toward royalties and an implicit understanding that Anderson would furnish a book a year—this was the bait with which Liveright tempted him. To leave Huebsch seemed to Anderson a retreat from the small-scale business methods of which he was fond, but Liveright's offer was too generous to be declined. Not without guilt, Anderson made the change, and from May 1925 until the end of 1927 enjoyed the security of a regular income. As it happened, the first of his books published by Liveright, *Dark Laughter*, sold some 50,000 copies and Liveright profited from his gamble. But Anderson found it increasingly difficult to turn out books at a rate that could earn him the advance he was receiving, and by the end of 1927 he owed Liveright $1200, a sum large enough to indicate that if he kept taking the weekly advance his debt would greatly increase. The checks soon became an intolerable pressure, and in a gesture of some courage he asked Liveright to cancel the arrangement. What had begun as a step toward security now seemed a sign of insecurity.

Meanwhile he was suffering other blows in his literary and personal life. In 1926 Ernest Hemingway, a rather promising young writer whom he had introduced to Gertrude Stein and had helped to find a publisher, issued a sad little book, *Torrents of Spring*, intended as a satire of Anderson and Stein. As Oscar Cargill has noted, this piece of literary cannibalism is actually a better burlesque of Hemingway's own work than of the writing of Anderson or Stein. Anderson kept a public silence about the book and if he ever replied directly to Hemingway's tasteless letter of "explanation" the reply is not known. (Stein, a patient and unforgetting warrior, repaid Hemingway with polemical interest in *The Autobiography of Alice B. Toklas* by needling his most vulnerable spot, his masculine pride.) In a letter to his brother Karl, Anderson remarked, correctly enough, that a brief satire of his work by Robert Benchley in a recent issue of *Life* had been funnier than Hemingway's book; but Hemingway's ineptness could hardly lessen the pain his attack caused Anderson, both as a blow from a friend and as a sign of the shifting critical attitude to his work.

Still more disturbing was a family crisis during the same year. Since late boyhood Anderson had hardly seen his brothers and had maintained close relations only with the kindly Karl, a portrait painter. But in the spring of 1926 he received a wire from Horace Liveright reporting that his youngest brother, Earl, who had drifted away from the family 15 years before, was now hospitalized in New York with a paralytic stroke. Earl's story, as he tearfully told it to Karl, was a poignant variation of the Joseph legend: A sensitive boy who felt himself an unwanted child and dreamed vaguely of an artistic career, Earl had deliberately cut himself off from his brothers as soon as they began to leave Clyde. At the time of his stroke he had been living in a lonely room in Brooklyn, working as a baker's helper and drawing sketches in his leisure. So strongly was the sense of failure rooted in him that he persistently avoided his brothers; once he had seen Sherwood walking along a New York street, had followed him in a state of great emotion, but had been unable to speak to him.

This story shook Sherwood: it aroused in him half-forgotten filial guilts, troubling memories of adolescence, confused feelings toward his family. He now began to draw somewhat closer to his brothers, particularly to Karl, and he wrote Earl a number of remarkable letters, in which loving warmth and an eagerness to recover the sense of brotherliness were mingled with a falsely oracular condescension. Earl's life seemed to him "a kind of living picture of all the more sensitive lives of our time," and at least in his imagination Sherwood responded lavishly to it. Yet after Earl's death in the spring of 1927 Sherwood found it possible to speak of him as a "mutt" and to strike a meticulously precise balance with Karl over expenses incurred during their brother's illness. Sherwood's affection was real enough, but so was his uncentered aggression toward his family, toward whatever or whoever raked up memories of the more painful parts of boyhood. At a time when he was trying to rechart his own life Sherwood was badly jarred by his youngest brother's appearance, for it dragged from the cellar of memory the old hurts of a boy who had never been able to articulate his love for his mother or quite decide what he felt about his father.

None of these troubles was in itself critical, but all of them together, particularly since they occurred during the decay of his third marriage, made for a pervasive if still modulated malaise. To regain a sense of purpose Anderson took a sharp turn in his life during 1926 and 1927, and only after that turn proved a partial failure did his malaise break out into acute crisis.

In the summer of 1925 when the prospect of the New Orleans heat seemed intolerable, Anderson and his wife spent a long vacation in the hilly southwest of Virginia. For two dollars a day they boarded in the village of Troutdale with an hospitable and quite well-educated family, the Greears, who soon became their good friends. After working a few hours each morning on *Tar* Anderson would toss horseshoes or play "flinch" and "setback" with the Greear boys, make friends with the neighboring farmers, and explore the gentle terrain he would later describe as "Claude Lorrain hills." Only after a while did the Greears discover that he was a famous writer, but to a family that even in its poverty proudly clung to its "old classics" and to the novels of John Fox, Jr. and Mrs. Humphry Ward, this was all the more reason for admiring its guest. In a charming memoir Mrs. Greear has told how Anderson brightened her family's life, once hiring cars for a trip to a circus and another time joining the boys in a possum hunt. "Mr. Anderson fitted right into our family life and made us feel easy about everything. . . . I got the notion that his wife was determined to make the best of us, since it seemed to suit him to be there. She was always nice, kind and pleasant in every way but was not so easy to know."

The Troutdale region seemed so lovely to Anderson that he decided to make it his permanent home. The need for a base to set out from, and return to, on his wanderings through the country had been growing in him; it was an equivalent of his need for a new motivating principle that could guide and control his work. In *Dark Laughter* he had already expressed his disillusionment with urban Bohemia and his wish to return to the apparently simpler life of the town. Now, among the Virginia mountain people—independent, dignified, and seldom split into "aristocrat" and poor white—he hoped to find the home he had not had for at least a decade, and with it a sense of place and participation.

With the money he made from his lectures and from *Dark Laughter*, Anderson bought a farm in a valley above Troutdale and began to build a house. Called Ripshin after a creek it borders, the house was made entirely from local field stone by mountain masons and carpenters. The wood was hewn by mountain craftsmen, and a large central fireplace and chimney were raised stone by stone. The house itself has a rare unconventional beauty: its walls one and a half feet thick, the main living room 30 feet long, the master bedroom graced with a large stone fireplace and a powerful stone arch, the floors of heavy broad-board, hand-fitted oak, and at its rim a stoned terrace. To Anderson, who hated the shoddiness of mass-production, this house seemed both a triumph of craftsmanship and a realization of his most intimate values: the very job of building it, interrupted by occasional carousals of the workmen, was a source of great pleasure to him. When the house was finished he could feel, as he later wrote in his *Memoirs*, that

> It was a place for my books. It was a place to come and to bring my friends. It was, I thought, a beautiful house and in building it I had got into a new relationship with my neighbors. . . . I was no longer a man apart, a writer, a something strange to them. I was just a man, like themselves. I had a farm. . . . I had found my land.

In the fall of 1927 Anderson took an even more decisive step to join himself to his new community: he bought, with funds advanced him by Burton Emmett, two weekly newspapers in the nearby town of Marion, the *Smyth County News* and the *Marion Democrat*. The papers would be an honorable way of earning a living; they would help him gain once more an intimate perspective on ordinary American life; and perhaps they could bring him closer to his two sons, Robert and John, whom he had recently discovered as grown young men and whom he hoped to involve in his new enterprise.

To enlarge the consciousness of his readers and yet avoid editorial dogmatism, Anderson confined himself mainly to local reporting, impressionistic sketches, and informal essays. As journalism, small-town or not, these pieces were often very good: they were warm, they tried to penetrate surfaces, they had a sly humor, and they avoided the stance of impersonal omniscience. Instead of syndicated boilerplate, Anderson used short-story classics to fill space. His political editorials (one paper was Democratic and the other Republican) were farmed out to party agents. Using either his own name or such pseudonyms as "Buck Fever," Anderson wrote most of the local material himself: a radiant sketch of a mountain dance; an amusing report of a mass excavation to find a missing man; an obituary for the printshop cat; mild crusades to clean up the town jail, build a new Negro school, outfit the town band; precise technical advice on how to pick mushrooms. In those of his pieces where he wrote as a reporter he came off quite well, but when he indulged himself in whimsy or heavy thinking he usually succumbed to the stereotypes of folksiness. Writing about Negroes was a problem, and while he was often generous and never sank to the level of other Southern editors he wrote things that are hardly tributes to his courage or intelligence: "the blacks remain children," "As for the negro, I am sure he is better off in the south than in the north. There, at least, injustice is often tempered by real affection."

His papers could have provided Anderson with a fair living and a placid life, for he soon became a town figure, liked and admired by the men he "wrote up" and pitched horseshoes with and tried to educate a bit. But while the papers may have offered a solution to his problems as a man who wanted to earn his bread honestly and in a congenial environment, they offered no solution to his problems as an artist reaching an impasse in his work. What he wrote for his papers was better than most of what appeared in the American press and it might well have satisfied Sherwood Anderson the country editor— but could it satisfy the man who had written *Winesburg, Ohio* and *The Triumph of the Egg*?

Certainly, little that he wrote or published between 1925 and the Depression could, or should, have given him much cause for satisfaction. Only the story "Death in the Woods" which appeared in a 1926 number of *The American Mercury* was first-rate; the remainder was fugitive journalism or, when more seriously intended, symptomatic of a loss of creative power. His books kept coming out regularly, about one a year, but they had depressingly little to say. In 1926 he published *Tar*, a fictional memoir of childhood, and *Sherwood Anderson's Notebook*, a collection of magazine pieces written several years earlier; in 1927 came *A New Testament*, his second effort at verse and no more successful than the first one; and in 1929 a group of his newspaper pieces, *Hello Towns*. Except for the story "A Meeting South" and flitting sketches of Ring Lardner and Gertrude Stein, the *Notebook* can interest no one but Anderson's biographers. *A New Testament* was an attempt to articulate basic life-attitudes, and there is something moving in the sight of an imagination wrestling with its inner inarticulateness, straining to release the seething at its core. "I would go under fields that are plowed. I would creep down the black fields. I would go softly, touching and feeling my way. I would be little brother to a kernel of corn that is to feed the bodies of men." In such images of self-immolation Anderson tried to express both his personal and his creative yearnings, but nothing in the book answered or even objectively embodied those yearnings.

Of the books written in these years only *Tar* makes a certain appeal to the imagination, but more than any of Anderson's works of fiction it justifies the critical commonplace that while he attracts sensitive adolescents he cannot satisfy the mature mind. Read at the age of sixteen the book seems a haunting and marvelously true portrait of American boyhood, faithful to the pathos of adolescent reverie. Reread in later years *Tar* still has patches of beauty, still manages an occasional entry into childhood feeling or a touch of that charcoal quaintness which is Anderson's forte. But *Tar* is fatally jolted by an uncertainty of perspective: Anderson writes well when he loses himself in his boy, but too often he is unwilling to take imaginative risks, he must reassert his adult presence and thereby destroy the tonal unity of the book. Despite its authentic moments *Tar* testifies to the weariness of an imagination aware that it is becoming a burden on its own past.

In mid-January 1929 Anderson's third marriage came to an abrupt and unpleasant end. Of all his marriages this one seems to have been the least generated by authentic emotional need; at its very beginning it had shown signs of strain. In the fall of 1924 Anderson was writing to Paul Rosenfeld from New Orleans, "Elizabeth went into business here. I want her out." He did indeed "want her out," but simultaneously he could not help wishing that her venture into interior decorating might provide some financial help and thereby release him from the need to write rapidly. During a short trip to Europe in the winter of 1927 Anderson became further irritated by what he took to be Elizabeth's excessive gentility— the very quality that had attracted her to him but now goaded him into feelings of inferiority; he was annoyed when she assumed the role of cultural mentor, when he contrasted her fluent French with his inept handling of the language. Back home Anderson released some of his resentment in jocular guise by referring to her as the "Morals Editor" of his papers. And though Elizabeth had been instrumental in designing Ripshin, he felt vaguely uneasy about what seemed to him her pretensions to becoming a country lady.

But these clashes of social attitude, reflecting disparities of education and upbringing, could hardly have been the major cause of their separation. Closer to that major cause, if one can ever be isolated, was Anderson's feeling that Elizabeth, in her personal relations, tended to coldness. In "Thanksgiving," a story he wrote in the early 'thirties but did not publish, he released—or betrayed—his innermost resentments. The story, which has an acerb quality seldom present in Anderson's work, describes the breakdown of Frank Blandin's marriage to Alice West, "a sweet enough slender little thing" who had approached love "with something of the air of the lamb being led to the slaughter." To see if a reconciliation is possible, Frank visits the Wests. (The Pralls lived in California.) Attenuated, genteel, and patronizing, the Wests suffer from "a queer separation from all real life" and from a strong inclination toward an inbreeding of affection: Alice's shoulders are frequently caressed by her older sister and Alice herself has "troubled dreams" in which her brother becomes a horse intent on destroying her. In this uncomfortable atmosphere the "pagan" Frank decides to end the marriage. The story closes with a harsh thrust: "If the woman, Alice, couldn't get him it didn't mean she was a blank. She had so evidently got her sister."

It is not at all necessary to take this story as a literal report in order to see it as a reflection of Anderson's bitterness about his marriage. That its breakup was not entirely Elizabeth's fault he readily acknowledged; in view of his own peccadillos he could hardly have done less.

But what bothered him most was his suspicion that a pattern ran through the continued failure of his marriages. In his *Memoirs* he had given one version of what he thought that pattern might be: "My first three marriages each lasted exactly five years. I have always been sure that none of the women were to blame. . . . Any practitioner of the arts is a trial to live with." Perhaps so; but the explanation is too comfortably general to explain or even usefully describe the specific failure of Anderson's marriages.

Though Anderson cultivated an image of himself as a man deeply responsive to the "pagan" and the sensual, in his first three marriages he had always turned to women who, whatever their virtues of character, could hardly have been described as either "pagan" or sensual. The women he wished to marry were earnest, ambitious, and inclined to be possessive; they were women able to manage him. Up to a point Anderson wished to be managed because it disposed of inconvenient responsibilities; less consciously, this wish was an expression of a desire to recreate in his maturity the family relations of his boyhood. That his women tended to starkness of appearance, that they were in various ways strong-willed, that they yearned to improve and elevate him—all this made it possible for Anderson to think of them in terms derived from his boyhood feelings for his mother. But at the same time he rebelled against the reappearance of the mother-figure; he desired women who would be beautiful, carefree, and playful, who would neither manage nor coddle him, who would provide through sexuality a realization of—and thereby a break from—the psychic tie which was the basis of his ideal image of woman. While the similarities in character and appearance which he sensed between his mother and his wives were strong enough to lead him into marriage, they were for that very reason not strong enough to keep him there.

Caught in the familiar conflict between the boyhood image of the mother-wife and the adult wish for an exciting mate, Anderson discharged his tensions in two characteristic ways. He moved restlessly from woman to woman, wife to wife, and he cultivated intense friendships with men. In one of his notebooks he wrote, "Perhaps in some essential part of me—never in the flesh—I have, all my life, loved men more than I have ever loved women." It is possible to honor completely the emphasis enclosed by dashes and yet see in this remark a key to the psychic difficulties which caused his marriages to fail. Consider the evidence: repeated expressions of aggression toward his father, an intense and guilt-burdened love for his mother, numerous references in his books to unfulfilled sexuality, three marriages to mother-wives and then rebellions against them, strong spiritual attachments to male friends —are not these the traits of that psychic configuration classically described as oedipal?

At a time when both his marriage and his writing were collapsing, none of Anderson's urges to health—his absorption in his papers, his growing love for his rediscovered sons, his selfless friendships with a number of young painters whom he helped in many ways—could long subsist. After ceding the active editorship of the papers to his son Robert in early 1929, Anderson had little left but gloomy isolation and purposeless drifting. From this point on, his drop into chaos is frighteningly sharp and fast. A quick trip to Chicago presumably to "gather material," a visit to a young painter in upstate New York, a jittery stay in Florida at the end of the year—and in between them lonely weeks in Virginia, "haunted by my failure to make it go with E." In the spring of 1929 Anderson writes his friend Ferdinand Schevill, "poor E. is very nice—much nicer than I will ever be—and I do not want her anymore. C. and T. were nice too. Why should I not face myself—a wanderer." In April he informs Horace Liveright that he has completed 15,000 words on a new novel, probably an early version of *Beyond Desire*, but that he has gone to pieces physically. In June he writes Schevill, "To tell the truth I have been this year more dispirited than I ever remember to have been . . . have lived on here, having my son with me, fighting constantly the impulse to flee. . . ." And to Robert he sends a long, touching, distraught letter trying to explain what has happened to him: "I had a world and it slipped away from me."

In December came another blow: news of the death of Tennessee, her body rotting for several days in the room where she had died. "Not just knowing what an ex-husband's status is," Anderson decided not to go to the funeral. When he heard the news, he wrote Schevill, "I thought of death all the time . . . wanted suicide." And on December 27 he sent a wire to Horace Liveright which reads like a concise and, in its final phrase, mordantly ironic summary of his condition: "Will have to withdraw promise of the novel for this spring stop happenings in my own life have upset me and I will have to have time to gather myself together stop anyway it is not a good piece of work stop forgive my being oversure."

Final Wanderings

A S HE continued to brood over the decline of both his personal relations and his creative powers, Anderson sensed that he could save himself only by finding some objective interest in the outer world, some valid deflection from his disturbed self. In 1930 that interest could hardly be anything but the social crisis seeping through the country, though the intensity with which he now turned to it was due, he said, to "another woman [who] came along and got at me in a new way." As he wrote to his brother Karl a year later:

It is rather strange how much I am influenced by women. They are such an important and necessary part of my life. Another woman came along and got at me in a new way. This wasn't an amorous matter. She felt, I think, that I was wasting myself so she got ahold of me rather for a purpose of her own. She felt, being a woman of brains and purpose, that the writers here in America were overlooking one of the biggest phases of American life, the factories. No one was going into the factories . . . seeing modern machinery at first hand, noting its effect on men etc. and she got me interested. . . . It gave me a new grip on life . . .

The woman was Eleanor Copenhaver, a social worker raised in a cultivated Marion family and now active in the Southern labor movement. By the spring of 1930 Anderson was advising a friend that he was again in love. He did not marry Eleanor Copenhaver until three years later, but in the meantime she profoundly changed the direction of his life: she accompanied him on trips through the South, persuaded him to study the life of the mill towns, and brought him into close relations with striking mill workers.

During the early 'thirties the textile workers' union was leading a number of desperate strikes in the South, and Anderson soon found himself speaking at mill-town strike rallies. By the usual standards he was an inept orator, yet he managed to reach a quick and intimate rapport with his audiences. Many of these workers had only recently come to the mill towns, and they felt he was instinctively turning to the back-country language that was their own. Thoroughly plebeian in spirit, Anderson did not need to guard against the condescension almost inevitable when an intellectual tries to communicate with workers; these were people he could immediately understand, the sort of men and women who had long moved through his books and who were now his neighbors in Virginia. (His condescension was reserved for more sophisticated audiences, toward whom he sometimes assumed a deliberately magnified naïveté.) And because he spoke to the mill workers in the language of unqualified fraternity he could also suggest, by muted indirection or by a mere gesture, that in their struggle they should look for something beyond the immediate need, something that might yield them a sense of genuine self-realization.

To Anderson these inarticulate and inexperienced strikers could never be subsumed under some abstraction of potential social power; unlike so many of the intellectuals then turning to radicalism he had no need to romanticize or idealize the workers—he saw them as they were and as they were he valued them. When he joked with a girl striker or gravely conversed with an older worker, there radiated from him a warmth, which some years later, in the vastly different circumstances of a New York literary party, would be seen by Lionel Trilling as "a certain serious interest he could have in the person he was shaking hands with or talking to for a formal moment . . . a certain graciousness or gracefulness which seemed to arise from an innocence of heart." And when he tried to express his feelings for the mill workers, Anderson wrote about those qualities in their lives which few trade unionists or radicals would have thought to notice. "There is a way in which people, workers, when they go on strike, even when they are pretty sure to lose, get something. . . ." In the mills they are dominated by "a big, tightly organized thing. It makes them feel small. They lose the sense of each other." But then a strike comes and "for a time at least, they get a rather fine feeling of each other. . . . Hands reach out. . . . Why, they are people in love with each other. . . ."

With a sensitivity rare at any time but particularly rare in the 1930's, Anderson measured the social distance between the workers and those who came from the "outside" to help them:

They crowd into the little halls. They cheer you when you come in. Faces peer up at you. There is hope, love, expectation in the eyes of the people. . . . A thousand eyes looking up at you. A kind of love grips you at the throat, but how utterly futile you feel, how ashamed. They so believe in you, or in someone like you, some talker, some writer, some leader. . . . You say a few words. You go away. You go back to your hotel. Some man comes in and offers you a drink. . . .

Not many of the radical intellectuals in the 1930's would have quite understood what Anderson meant when he said he was "ashamed," not many were so delicately aware of the temptations latent in their idealism. As he traveled through the South, Anderson increasingly identified himself with the mill workers, and sometimes that identification touched on his most intimate memories. "In some queer way," he wrote to his brother Karl, "I always see mother in these factory women and want to fight for them."

The Anderson of these years appears at his best in his restless sense of responsibility to the mill workers. During one of the textile strikes he wrote to Edmund Wilson that he had a "guilty feeling just now about taking any part in pulling people out on strike. We go and stir them up. Out they come and presently get licked. Then we go comfortably off. It seems to me that if we . . . are to go in at all with the workers perhaps we should be ready to go all the way. I mean that we should be willing to go live with them in their way and take it in the neck with them." Anderson's idea of "going to the people" was not carefully thought out (otherwise he would have been quick to see its perils), but his motivation in making it was wholly praiseworthy, particularly when compared with the manipulative attitudes that radical intellectuals were then often showing toward the workers.

By 1931 Anderson had openly declared himself a radical. When Theodore Dreiser was indicted on charges of criminal syndicalism during a coal miners' strike in Harlan County, Kentucky, Anderson told a New York protest meeting: "Let's have more criminal syndicalism." Writers, he said, should "line up with the underdogs" and stop worrying about their reputations. But then he indulged in one of those muddled political statements that would be all too typical of his new radicalism: What, he asked, is the difference between a Communist and a Socialist? "I guess the Communists mean it." To his immediate audience this seemed a remarkably good answer, but if Anderson had been pressed to explain precisely what the Communists meant and the Socialists did not, he would have been in a most uncomfortable position. For there is no evidence that he had ever troubled to find out.

In the spring of the following year Anderson gave his name to a manifesto, "Culture and the Crisis," in which a number of intellectuals declared their radicalism and endorsed the Communist candidate for President, William Z. Foster. To Edmund Wilson, who had asked him to sign it, Anderson wrote, "I wouldn't mind saying Wilson to you that if at any time anything comes up like this manifesto and my name has any value you are at liberty to use it. Where you are willing to go I'll go." Anderson's compliment to Wilson was impressive, but his blithe readiness to commit his signature to documents unseen and unwritten hardly promised the responsibility necessary for his new political commitment.

A few months later Anderson joined a group of literary men—Waldo Frank, James Rorty, Elliot Cohen—in a protest against the use of federal troops during the bonus march. When the protesters arrived at the White House, the President, as the *New York Times* chastely reported, "was too busy to see them," but their visit helped dramatize popular resentment at the way the veterans had been treated. A few weeks later, in an "open letter" to President Hoover which was printed in *The Nation*, Anderson wrote:

> I came to you with the other writers because I was ashamed not to come. When men are trying to assert their rights to live decently in America . . . when these men are brutally put down by police or soldiers —bear in mind I have seen these things with my own eyes—when that happens something within me hurts and bleeds.

The "open letter" was an extremely effective piece of propaganda, and the considerable praise it received encouraged Anderson to plunge deeper into radicalism. In the fall of 1932 he went as an American delegate to the "Amsterdam Peace Congress," one of the innumerable gatherings of the innocent arranged by the not-so-innocent, and wrote home that he found it "very exciting" and "rather gorgeous." During the same year he began to write for the *New Masses* and participated in its symposium on "How I Came to Communism." His hope for the future, he said in another *New Masses* article, rested on "the fighting young Communists" among whom "I found poverty, youth, no gloom."

But even as he was being drawn into the Stalinist cultural orbit, it was greatly to Anderson's credit that he instinctively clung to a sober view of the problem endlessly debated in the left-wing literary journals: the relation of the sympathetic writer to the radical movement.

In the *New Masses* he wrote that "revolutionists will get the most help out of such men as myself not by trying to utilize [us] as writers of propaganda but in leaving us as free as possible to strike, by our stories out of American life, into the deeper facts." Obviously sensible though this remark was, it completely denied the current Stalinist position on literature, and had it been made by a writer of smaller reputation it might well have evoked the party's corrective wrath. But Anderson was too valuable a "name" to be chastised for a mere deviation from the path of "proletarian literature."

Anderson's radicalism had never been secured in a theory of society or a clear vision of the goal to which he had publicly committed himself. Initially and at its best, his radicalism was a generous response to the misery he had seen while traveling through the country—and since it seemed to him that the Communists alone really cared about that misery he accepted them as his natural allies. Once, however, there appeared in the New Deal a hope for a social amelioration more immediate and less troublesome than that offered by the radicals, Anderson was quick to accept it. The relation of the New Deal to capitalist society as a whole was a problem that seems to have troubled him little more than the relation of Stalinist totalitarianism to the radical values it claimed to embody.

When Anderson began to modify his radical views there were no distinct or dramatic steps to disillusionment, no declarations of opinion for public interest or private satisfaction. But when Paul Rosenfeld wrote an article in *Scribner's* attacking the radical intellectuals for "a blind abandonment of the historic cause and faith and object that have always been the artist's," Anderson was provoked into a certain self-consciousness about his gradually changing attitudes. He might with some justice dismiss Rosenfeld's own position as an esthete's complacence, but it was quite another thing to question Rosenfeld's charge that most of the writers who aligned themselves with the Communist Party surrendered their intellectual independence and that in the name of revolutionary necessity they grossly, even masochistically, denied artistic standards. When he wrote a personal reply to the article, Anderson was both apologetic and self-indulgent: "It may be that I got reckless. After all Paul you have to trust someone. I am not a politically-minded man." It simply did not occur to Anderson—as it did not occur to other literary men far more deeply committed to radicalism —that anyone who engages in political activity must be ready to accept political responsibility.

During the next few years there was little responsibility and not much more dignity in Anderson's political behavior. In 1936 he sent the Russian news agency, Tass, a message worthy of the later Sidney Webb: "The new Soviet constitution seems to me to wipe out the stock criticism against the USSR that the intellectual life of a great nation has been stultified." Yet during the same period he could also suggest to a magazine editor an article about "the essential and rather pathetic romanticism of the radical . . . most of them are essentially such children face to face with the facts." It is hard to determine which of these two pronouncements is more distasteful: the endorsement of Stalin's "constitution" or the condescension toward "the radical," obviously inferior to Anderson as a *Realpolitiker*.

Had Anderson frankly declared that he was changing

his mind about communism, he would have been open to attack only on the grounds of opinion. But his radical friends suspected that he was now trying, perhaps without full self-awareness, to wriggle out of his own past, and they were certainly justified in reacting with some bitterness to an article he wrote for a 1933 issue of *The New Yorker*, in which he adopted that magazine's posture of amused superiority while retelling his story as a White House protester. "We had been asked, pleaded with, to go down there, and we went. When we got there, we felt silly, at least I did." Why Anderson should have felt silly about pleading for the bonus marchers he did not say, nor did he explain why he had failed to mention this feeling in his *Nation* article a year earlier. Instead, he offered the defense soon to become habitual with jolted fellow-travelers: "You get caught. . . . We who do the protesting are seldom taken into the confidence of the men who run such affairs."

Anderson was here falling back on the assumption that had impoverished so much of his intellectual life: the assumption of innocence, the assumption that the writer is exempt from responsibility for his commitments because he is not a "politically-minded man" or, in more general terms, because his role is merely to serve as a passive recipient of impressions from his environment. The same assumption had pervaded his relation to the "Chicago Renaissance," when he had been innocent of the cultural past he disregarded; it was present in his relation to the 1920's, when he was innocent of the complications in the sexuality he invoked, and had passages from *Dark Laughter* been thrown up to him he would have pleaded, with genuine dismay, the very same innocence. When he began to write for *The New Masses* he did not bother to examine the nature of Stalinism, and when he ceased writing for it he did not publicly ask whether a rejection of Stalinism necessarily involved a rejection of social radicalism. When he praised Stalin's "constitution" he did not think to inquire about its effect on the actuality of Russian life, and when he complained that he had been "used" by the party's agents he did not ask whether he might be responsible for having allowed himself to be "used."

In the end all that he salvaged from his radical experience was his never-diminished feeling for the Southern workers. It was this feeling which had once led him to write to a union leader: "I think it would be infinitely better in all cases to be perfectly frank with the workers. When they are licked tell them so. Treat them like grown men and women. Great God they have been patronized enough." By comparison with the ungenerous memories so many intellectuals would soon have of their radical interlude, Anderson's sense of plebeian fraternity seems a precious saving.

The tone of plebeian fraternity, of easy and spontaneous friendliness, sustains the best of the journalistic pieces Anderson wrote during the early 'thirties. In *The American Country Fair*, a short sketch issued as a limited edition in 1930, that tone is employed for a pleasant exercise in nostalgia. Somewhat wishfully, Anderson describes the fair as "a pagan outburst" in a dry land. The girls "walk boldly. Now is the time to get yourself a man." The men "act a little puzzled. They wander about." At the climax of the fair, businessmen and doctors, farmers and mechanics "put on little gaily colored caps and gaily colored coats" to race their trotters. Anderson is thoroughly at home here: few other American writers have ever reported the small town's pleasures with such affection and authority. But soon the sketch breaks off—it is only a fragment, a fragile daguerreotype of yesterday.

In *Perhaps Women*, a book of speculations on the mill towns published in 1931, there is the same concern with the quality of the life ordinary Americans lead, this time unsoftened by nostalgia but still sympathetic and gentle. The best things in the book come in intuitive flickers: late at night two mill girls laugh with sly sexual pride as they walk past Anderson, a mill owner defends the drabness of his town in terms remarkably like those used by apologists for the totalitarian state, and in a sudden breakthrough to awareness Anderson notes the "queer vicarious sense of power . . . of false power . . . scattered everywhere through the American world now." The one completely effective chapter, "Loom Dance," is a swift, insinuatingly rhythmic impression of a mill workers' rebellion against the speed-up. A weaver sees an efficiency expert clock his wife as she goes to the toilet, and in a howl of rage he begins to dance a compulsive imitation of the loom he tends.

> . . . He hopped up and down in an absurd jerky way. Cries, queer and seemingly meaningless cries, came from his throat.
> He danced for a moment like that and then he sprang forward. He knocked the minute-man down. Other

weavers, men and women, came running. Now they were all dancing up and down. Cries were coming from many throats. . . .

> The [minute-man's] glasses had fallen on the floor.
> His watch had fallen on the floor.
> All the looms in the room kept running.
> Lights danced in the room.
> The looms kept dancing.
> A weaver was dancing on a minute-man's watch.
> A weaver was dancing on a minute-man's glasses.
> Other weavers kept coming.
> They came running. Men and women came from the spinning room.
> There were more cries.
> There was music in the mill.

Had Anderson confined himself to such sketching, his book could have been a valuable impression of the new industrial South. But *Perhaps Women* is also a book with an insistent thesis, which for Anderson is almost always an occasion for trouble. In *Perhaps Women* he advanced the theory that "modern man is losing his ability to retain his manhood in the face of the modern way of utilizing the machine and that what hope there is for him lies in women." For this notion Anderson was mercilessly ridiculed by a good many critics; indeed, if one demands from it the operative precision of a scientific theory one can only conclude that it is absurd. Why are women less susceptible to the blight of impotence than men? Do women in fact resist mechanization more than men? And if they do, how does Anderson propose they master the machine-world which is enfeebling their mates? Though never raised in the book, such questions must occur to every reader of *Perhaps Women*. Having committed the indiscretion of advancing an abstract idea, Anderson would not so

far forget himself as to support it with organized and veri-
fiable propositions.

But is this all? Can nothing be salvaged? Is the book
merely an exercise in sentimental phallicism? Anderson's
thesis, as thesis, hardly warrants serious discussion, but if
one troubles to undercut the literal surface of his meaning one finds that in his own way he arrived at a central
insight into modern life—that the factory system tends to
reduce men to a function and thereby drain them of their
human inwardness. He expressed this insight in too pa-
rochial a vocabulary, he lacked the cultural sophistication
to consider its attendant complications. Nor could the condition he noticed be restricted to men in as literal a
manner as he did—it was rather a pervasive impotence
before the emotional possibilities of life, a failure of both
sexes to achieve human personality, a loss of dignity and
selfhood. But no matter how fragmentary and misshapen,
Anderson's insight is crucial to an understanding of American life, and in an occasional flare it breaks through the
book with a rightness and immediacy few American
writers can equal.

It is this insight unencumbered by theory which
makes so valuable Anderson's second book of journalism
in the 1930's. To be sure, *Puzzled America* has the faults
one soon comes to expect in Anderson's reportage: the
self-imitation ("warm days of doing nothing . . . listening to voices in Mobile streets"), the manipulation of
sentiment, the pathetic eagerness to be impressed by poli-
ticians with a Populist vocabulary, the inclination to replace concrete observation with ingrown conceits. When
the book came out in 1935 it received considerable and
rather caustic notice in the radical press, perhaps because

it said what most radicals preferred not to hear: that there was no longer a chance in depression America, if there had ever been one, for a revolution. One anonymous Marxist reviewer did, however, recognize part of its value. Writing in the *New International* he chastised Anderson for his slothful manner of handling ideas: "We find *Puzzled America* shot through with what might be called social sentimentality, just as his earlier books were clouded by a special kind of sexual sentimentality. . . . [This] accounts for the emergence of the C.C.C., Rush Holt and Floyd Olson as the heroes of the book." But the reviewer did credit Anderson with accurately observing "the unstable, directionless mood that now possesses the country . . . as we read on, the mood becomes more closely defined: it is not hopeless, but confused; it is not exhausted, but rather waiting; it is neither revolutionary nor conservative, but so far without formulated goal or aim."

But even this perceptive critic did not see what is most distinctive in *Puzzled America,* something other than its indulgence in social sentimentality or its useful graphing of social moods. *Puzzled America* is one of the few books that convey a sense of what it meant to live in depression America, one of the few books in which authentic and anonymous voices rise to tell the cost of joblessness and Southern share-cropping and Northern foreclosures. Occasionally Anderson gets in the way of his story with a tricky ending or a bit of obviously "understated" pathos, but in the main *Puzzled America*, like Edmund Wilson's *The American Jitters,* is a collection of depression reportage that outlives its immediate preoccupations. Anderson had little of Wilson's gift for tenaciously accumu-

lating social details or illuminating neglected social crevices; his reportorial style, by comparison with Wilson's,
was meager and provincial; but he nevertheless edged
into the feelings of the people with whom he talked in a
way Wilson seldom did. (In his journalism, where he
was under no obligation to be literary, Anderson had a
far better ear for dialogue than in his novels.)

People flit through *Puzzled America*, seen briefly but
in sharp focus: What did the Communist girl want in the
mill town? "Most of all, to get into jail," laughs a miner.
"I'd never been a tramp, but I became one," says an
electrician, "you can get a new picture of life." A tobacco farmer complains: "It's really a woman's crop. . . .
You've got to mess and mess with it, all year long." For
the tobacco men things are going badly: "We've got
pretty puny trying to help ourselves." And in a Southern
town Anderson is told by a sick worker, "I never will
succeed. I might as well be put out of the way."

The most moving voices, from "A Union Meeting,"
are recorded by Anderson with a tender, trembling simplicity. A strike has been lost. Three hundred of the
thousand workers, "their most active union members,"
are now without work, unwanted by the mill. A union
delegation has been to see the mill manager, but he
promises nothing. In tedious, fumbling phrases Brother
Hadley reports on the visit—what the young man in the
office said, how the manager's secretary was "frightened,"
everything but what his listeners strain to hear. A collection is taken up for one of the men. Brother Hadley
hesitates, doesn't know how to end. "It may be," he says,
"you ought to have another delegation, another leader,
some one else to do your talking." There is silence, noth-

ing to say. Brother Hadley cries out fiercely, "I wasn't afraid of him." But Sister Smedly, sitting alone up front, senses the full hopelessness of the meeting. "I can't make no report," she says.

If taken as a work of impressionistic sociology, *Puzzled America* can be read as a portrait of depression America and as a study of dislocations following the invasion of capitalist economy in the South. Here "a new dominant economic class [is] springing up . . . hard new little tyrants" who "would make money in hell." Here are the ghastly mill towns, the hill men wandering through lonely industrial valleys, the pathetic efforts at unionization. And all the while Anderson keeps watching and hoping, a good man whose sympathy keeps him going even when his mind stalls. A labor leader asks him whether he "wants in" to a union meeting—

> Yes, of course. I want in everywhere. To go in is my aim, I want into fashionable hotels and clubs, I want into banks, into people's houses, into labor meetings, into courthouses. . . .

> I did not say all this. "Sure," I said.

Though it brought him partial satisfactions and an indispensable income, journalism was hardly the end for which Anderson lived. Unless *Tar* be considered a novel, he had published no work of fiction since *Dark Laughter* and that was a book which belonged to a rejected past. (Freud, he told a friend, "took us all in.") In the late 1920's he made several efforts to complete novels: *Another Man's House* announced "in preparation" and *Beyond Desire* several times begun and dropped. The first of these books never did appear but the second, after much revision, came out in 1932.

Beyond Desire—there is no point in being euphemistic—is a work of incoherence. Its structure is a chaos: time sequences jumbled, minor characters granted distracting flashbacks, an entire section quite unrelated to the central plot thread. Its prose is in an advanced stage of decomposition: phrases dangling without support, a desperate reliance on ellipsis, sentences that jar and grate in their false naïveté. And its theme—the effort to find a goal beyond desire—soon becomes a sad botch: there is no controlling point of view, no guiding intelligence, only the gesture of quest which has come to seem irresponsible and factitious because there is no genuine effort to find anything.

Beyond Desire is mainly the story of Red Oliver's seduction by the librarian of a Southern town. When she abandons him for a comfortable marriage, the dreamy young Oliver suspects that he has made the error of staking too much on sex. He drifts into a North Carolina town where the Communists are leading a strike, and in an act motivated neither by intellectual principle nor by emotional fellowship he defies a militia officer and is killed. Though a hero to the strikers, Red does not know why he submits to martyrdom, nor is he free, even at the moment before his death, of the desire he has presumably sought to overcome; he never achieves an active comprehension of himself or his relation to the world.

In the midst of this rambling narrative Anderson has inserted a long sketch called "Mill Girls," the one section of the book written with a certain creative economy and emotional conviction. But the novel proper is a compulsive accumulation of those witless maunderings which in his worst writing replace both sensuous impression and intellectual activity; here inarticulateness becomes a symptom of power and depth, of an inner wisdom too portentous to be committed to mere language.

Neither in his wretched little affair with the "emancipated" librarian nor in his arbitrary exposure to martyrdom does Red Oliver reach a sufficient level of consciousness to relate himself meaningfully to sex or to radicalism. The real problem of the book—as, before it, of *Marching Men* and *Many Marriages*—is the absurd disproportion between the serious themes which disturb Anderson and the mental sluggishness of the characters assigned to cope with them. "Red Oliver had to think. He thought he had to think. He wanted to think—thought he wanted to think. In youth there is a kind of hunger." It is completely characteristic of Anderson that he should sum up Oliver's "need" for thought in an organic, sexual image.

But it is the prose itself, the quality of the language, which best reveals the emaciation of Anderson's talent. In such vertiginous writing as this—

> She didn't think it definitely. She thought it. There was a feeling of being superior to the young men. It was nice. It wasn't nice . . .

—there emerges the failure of a writer; a writer who had to think, wanted to think, felt a kind of hunger, but had never really learned to think.

Beyond Desire marked Anderson's nadir as a writer of fiction, and he himself later spoke of it as a "defeat." His next novel, *Kit Brandon*, suggests the pathos, for those who care to see it, of a badly bewildered artist struggling to regain his creative authority. As it happens, most of the reviewers were by now too impatient with Anderson's predictable faults to notice that pathos.

For his portrait of Kit Brandon Anderson employed a technique new to him: he put himself directly into the book, the auditor recording Kit's story as she sits in his car and talks to him shyly. This is what she tells him: that as the daughter of a Blue Ridge moonshiner she quickly accepted the view that society is unremittently malevolent toward the weak; that she ran away from home when her father began to molest her; that for a time she worked in a mill where she dreamed of wealth and adventure; that she then married the ineffectual son of a bootlegger but found no inner satisfaction in her new luxury; and that she finally abandoned herself to lawlessness, becoming one of the most daring night drivers in the bootlegger's gang. Morally adrift now that the gang has been destroyed by the police, Kit emerges as a symbol of human desiccation, a poor-white sister of Fitzgerald's Gatsby and O'Hara's Gloria Wandrous. Like them she fears she has been deprived of the very essence of life, and like them she destroys herself through an excess of undirected and unmodulated energy. *Kit Brandon* is not nearly so good a novel as *The Great Gatsby* nor nearly so skillful a novel as *Butterfield 8*, but in its occasional moments of power Anderson perceives the moral uncertainty at the center of American life with a sureness quite as impressive as Fitzgerald's and completely free of O'Hara's truculent sensationalism.

Some of those occasional moments are very good indeed. The sense of place is fresher in *Kit Brandon* than

in any other Anderson novel except the first parts of
Windy McPherson's Son and *Poor White*: one credits the
existence of John Brandon's sodden farm, the gray mill
where Kit works, the farmhouse that is the gang's hide-
out, and the aura of desolate freedom in which Kit
speeds her night cargo. And though Anderson does not
establish Kit as a character in depth, he brings her to a
kind of synoptic reality through shrewd notations of her
dominant traits. He knows the precise mixture of scorn
and sympathy with which she will view attempts to un-
ionize the mill. He knows the hunger for experience that
beats within her—the hunger which drives her to imitate
the dress and manners of the middle class but which also
stirs in her a weird memory of the way a boy at the mill
went through an act one moonlit evening of prancing,
trotting, and neighing like a horse. Best of all, Anderson
knows the inverted relationship Kit will establish with
her car once she abandons hope in human relationships.
Having been unable to find gratification in her own sexual role, she gains through her wild driving a sense of
malelike mastery; the car becomes a sexual fetish and
her domination of it both a symbol of her scorn for men
and a surrogate for the love she has not had.

If, nevertheless, *Kit Brandon* remains an unsatisfactory novel, the trouble this time lies rather in technique
than in initial conception. Anderson's intrusions in the
opening chapters are effective in setting the novel's tone;
but as they continue and soon begin to destroy the possibility of dramatic accumulation, one fervently wishes he
would step out of his book. *Kit Brandon* has a number
of good scenes, but in the absence of the connective tis-

sues of narrative they remain mere isolated achievements.
Where Anderson should have been working up his story,
he ineffectually speculated on its significance.

In a letter to Maxwell Perkins, who was now his editor, Anderson wrote that he was trying to be "more objective, trying, you see, to use mind as well as feeling";
and the signs of that effort are visible throughout the
book, particularly in an occasional tightening of the prose.
Had *Kit Brandon* been written by a young man at the
beginning of his career, its faults might have seemed
minor blemishes easily removed by rigorous editing. But,
as Perkins must have realized, it was now too late for rigorous editing: what he had done for Wolfe it would be
impossible to do for Anderson. For when *Kit Brandon*
appeared in 1936 Anderson was nearly 60 years old—and
it was the last time he would offer a novel to public view.

Why does a writer continue to write once his gift has
withered, once he has himself become infected with the
fear that his best work is done and only failure can follow? The question is real enough for anyone trying to
understand why the early achievement of American
writers is so seldom enlarged in maturity; but for the
writer himself, for the actual living man who prepares
once more to test his talent as he wryly listens to the
funeral orations read over it, the question is not real—
how can it be? More than most writers of his generation,
Anderson could estimate quite precisely the value of any
of his works; in his genuinely serious moments he *knew*
that with a few exceptions his books had been diminish-
ing in quality since the early 'twenties. Yet his last years

are crowded with desperate and truncated efforts: plans drawn and unfulfilled, books begun and unfinished, books finished and unpublished.

But still: why did he continue? Perhaps, it may be suggested, there was now little else he could do. If that was a motive at all it was a very minor one, for when Henry Wallace offered him a job as a publicity writer in Washington, Anderson politely refused. He was indeed worried about earning a living ("I haven't made a cent since Mae West was a virgin") and he was particularly worried about his financial dependence on his wife, but he doggedly held to his status as a full-time literary man. For without that, would he be anything at all?

In a letter he wrote in 1939 Anderson recognized that the sheer fact of his writing had itself become a problem: he had to keep writing, he explained, because of his wife's unlimited faith in him. It is no discredit to Anderson that he was here almost certainly deceiving himself, for actually the need to write came from deep within his own being. What that need was is perhaps indicated by a few sentences written during the last year of his life but often anticipated in earlier years: "I am pretty sure that writing may be a way of life in itself. . . . I think the whole glory of writing lies in the fact that it forces us out of ourselves and into the lives of others. In the end the real writer becomes a lover."

Each morning, as he went to his work-cabin at Ripshin and "warmed up" by writing letters to his friends, he still hoped for that moment of profound release when the creative energy flows toward its proper object; and if such moments now came less frequently than they once had, if the agonies of composition and the extremities of his desire tricked him into seeing those moments when in fact they had not come, that was part of the risk he was ready to take. Being an artist was the one honorable way of living he knew, and his awe before that way of living was as intense now at Ripshin as it had been a quarter of a century before at Elyria. And then too, there was, no doubt, the secret hope that he would again find his authentic voice; the hope that from patience and labor would yet come a miraculous rebirth.

All of Anderson's friends knew that he was struggling with his daemon, though they sometimes saw quite different aspects of that struggle. To most of them he was still the Anderson they had always known, a man blessed with hope and laughter and curiosity; to one or two of them he seemed thoroughly defeated and resigned to defeat. There was a strand of truth in both views. Buoyed by his successful marriage and secure in Ripshin as never before, Anderson found many personal satisfactions in his last years; yet he also sensed that his creative life had gone dry and this knowledge brought him hours of terrible gloom. "I can't live," he cried out in a letter to Max Perkins, "by merely being thought of as a sometimes master of my craft"—and who can remain indifferent to the pain in that cry? The younger writers, he felt, were passing him by; the critics who had once been warm were now ungenerous and impatient; America did not remember.

It was galling, too, that of the handful of younger writers who did acknowledge him as a master, one, Thomas Wolfe, should be forced by some egocentric compulsion to quarrel with him needlessly and then brutally tell him he was "finished," and another, William

Saroyan, should be a writer whose work he considered false. In loneliness and doubt, sometimes with a mild bitterness, Anderson kept spurring his talent, and his disappointment came through, not in any public display or spectacular disintegration, but in a series of small yet symptomatic incidents.

In 1930 or perhaps somewhat earlier, Anderson was once approached by a man in a New Orleans restaurant and asked if he were a Mr. Smith. With a sudden bitterness that chilled his friends, Anderson replied, "No, but I wish I was."

Shortly after the publication of *Perhaps Women*, the *Nation* gave Anderson a party at a Greenwich Village restaurant. For a while he was at the center of conversation, but about midway in the party an unexpected guest, William Faulkner, came in. The two writers met and joked in a friendly manner, but when Faulkner, then a rising novelist, went to another part of the room, there was a movement of people after him. Almost alone in his corner, Anderson now sat quietly smiling, slowly and gently stroking a large hat he was holding, saying nothing but continually stroking the hat.

During the mid-'thirties Anderson kept working and hoping for a Broadway production of a dramatized version of *Winesburg* he had written with a "professional" collaborator. The play was done, apparently with some sensitivity, by Jasper Deeter's Hedgerow Theater in Philadelphia, was then optioned by the Theatre Guild, but never reached New York—a severe blow to what must have seemed a chance to revive former glories.

In 1936 Anderson wrote to Theodore Dreiser suggesting ways of breaking down the writer's loneliness: "We are too much separated. . . . I think it is our loneliness for each other that has made most of us throw too much on women. . . ."

And two years later that loneliness led him to write to many of his old friends—Brooks, Frank, Schevill, Rascoe, Stieglitz, and others—asking for their pictures to hang on the walls of his work room. "I get sometimes," he wrote to one of them, "a desperate feeling about life. . . ."

These incidents were indirect reflections of his disappointment and bewilderment; in his letters and in a pocket diary he kept during the last years of his life there are more direct reflections. He was then beginning and leaving unfinished novel after novel—*Brother Earl*, a fragmentary version of the life of his youngest brother; *A Late Spring*, a story about a man's effort "to get belief in himself"; and *How Green the Grass*, a portrait in several versions of a young man trying to become an artist. In 1937 Anderson was writing to his brother Karl: "I seem to be writing blind these days, putting down and putting down, without much form." The following year he wrote to Gertrude Stein: "I keep milking the cow but, just at present, I am waiting for the cream to rise." In another letter he wrote, "What I need, I know, is acceptance of defeat. . . ." And during these years his diary is full of notations of crisis:

I am in one of my stale periods. . . . Nothing I do has any meaning.

I have had to put this novel aside for the moment. . . . It is not rich enough. . . .

I have been depressed and unhappy about work.

It seems to me that I have done nothing.

. . . terribly depressing day—sunk in deep gloom—unable to work.

. . . [Writing is] ineffectual. . . .

. . . ineffectual. . . .

Still, in some ways Anderson was a happy man during these unfertile years. He would travel through the country with his wife, releasing again the *Wanderlust* deep within him; he would sometimes stay at the Hotel Royalton in New York where he enjoyed the Broadway atmosphere, met his old friends and worked, as he liked to, in a cramped hotel room, perhaps on his last project, the *Memoirs*. And then he would return to his home, to Ripshin, the "most beautiful house in America," where he acted the gracious host to the friends who journeyed down to see him, pretended to become something of a gentleman farmer, and traded secrets of wine-making with Andy Funk, the Marion lawyer who was one of the close friends of his last years. The Copenhaver family accepted him completely, and until her death his mother-in-law, Laura Copenhaver, was a friend who understood and helped him. His national reputation had declined, but to his friends in Marion he was still the famous writer who had honored them by becoming their neighbor.

Sherwood Anderson the man, insofar as he could be separated from Sherwood Anderson the writer, was happy. But there were layers of his personality, by no means the least significant, where such a separation was impossible. The clues to his inner feeling, the feeling beneath the joviality and kindness and charm, were small, but they were there to be seen. In the evenings, when he had guests at Ripshin, Anderson insisted they play croquet with him, a game of which he was passionately fond. Until dark, and sometimes even beyond dark with the aid of flashlights, he played croquet—in deep earnest, insistently eager to win.

On February 28, 1941 Anderson and his wife sailed for a tour of South America. Eight days later, in the hospital at Colón, Panama, he was dead. Aboard ship he had been stricken with an abdominal congestion and peritonitis, presumably the result of swallowing a toothpick while eating *hors d'œuvre*. Two weeks later his body was buried in a hill overlooking Marion.

Anderson as he was in his last months has been vividly sketched by his friend Roger Sergel:

> His clothes were careless then, and the necktie was no longer slipped through a ring. The rectangular face was still ruddy, but had softened toward the almost flabby; the chin was double—but still lifted in laughter as his head, with its thin gray hair, slanted away, and its little nod that expected agreement was often then a tremor. The eyes were the same, black and impenetrable and receiving—receiving you, receiving all and mingling us all with those dreams that came back changed into imperishable stuff about the boy who bragged at the races, the old woman who died in the woods, the sad hornblowers, and the man who late at night whispered into the telephone that life was sweet.

At the funeral his friends, from Marion and from the North, spoke of his literary achievement and of his resistance to "success." Theodore Dreiser sent a message: "To me, amidst all the strain of living and working, he was a comforting figure—never in any sense a slave to money, or that other seeming necessity to so many, show or pretense." But success—the success which Anderson, after Henry James, had called a bitch—could not be completely denied. No one would have understood better than Anderson the irony, even the ironic necessity, of the announcement in the Elyria *Chronicle-Telegram*: "Sherwood Anderson, Former Elyria Manufacturer, Dies."

An American as Artist

"F̲OR all my egotism," wrote Sherwood Anderson at
the end of his life, "I know I am but a minor
figure." This self-estimate is both accurate and sincere: it comes, in the *Memoirs*, directly after an eager
tribute to those writers of the past whom Anderson
most admired. Yet it was characteristic of his feeling for
the creative life that even when he was most humble
about his work he was proud to be doing it. In some
ways the minor artist needs the buttress of pride more
than the major one: he must believe that his career, in
its fragmentary achievement no less than its integrity of
conduct, is intrinsically worthy. This pride—the pride
which permits the minor artist to place himself in fraternal relation to past greatness even as he realizes the
limitations of his own work—Anderson had.

The pity of it was, however, that in his last years he
found it so hard to preserve that pride. How graciously
a culture accepts its minor artists is one gauge of its
health. A secure culture, organically related to its own
past and yet forever modulating it, will quickly assimilate
the minor artist's vision and will honor and bolster him

during his lifetime. But American culture—committed as it is to a highly competitive ethic, a systematic suspicion of the past, and an uneasy depreciation of the frankly minor work—could hardly bolster Anderson once his imagination had begun to falter. At first it overvalued him, perhaps even turned his head, and then it ignored him as if he were unobtrusively dead; but on neither occasion could it fortify his taste or direct him with affectionate severity to what was best in his work. It was a culture with a depressingly short memory and it behaved as if that short memory were its outstanding virtue; in its frenetic quest for novelty it was always searching for new heroes to elevate, always discarding artists as if they were bankrupts defeated by stronger rivals (its most favored author, Ernest Hemingway, saw literature as a vast boxing tournament), and always rediscovering artists who should never have been forgotten. In so discontinuous a culture a writer like Anderson, who had only a slight capacity for detachment or self-protection, was certain to be wounded as he had once been praised. It is for this reason, though hardly for this reason alone, that his literary career seems representative of the effort so many Americans have made to become artists.

It was the pattern of Anderson's life that he had always to resume it as if from afresh: he could not enjoy the kind of organic growth that an artist, or any other human being, should enjoy. For a man like Anderson, who drew so heavily from each immediate phase of the *Zeitgeist* because he could draw so little from anything else, each inevitable change in that *Zeitgeist* could only mean personal dislocation and crisis. The new begin-

ning, with guilt or error or failure forgiven, is a typical
daydream of Americans, a people convinced of its indestructible innocence or at least of the eternal possibility
of a painless redemption; the new beginning, with the
hero returning from fiasco to a wife-mother or mistress-
mother whom he serenely expects to be waiting for him,
is a pervasive theme in Anderson's books; and the new
beginning, each time somewhat further stripped of innocence, is a recurrent fact in Anderson's life. That it
was necessary and perhaps unavoidable in his life explains much about the fragmentary nature of his achiev-
ment.

It is here that the absence of an ample sense of tradition exacts its price—tradition not as a fashionable catalogue of great names or titles, but as the whole of those
inherited resources by which a writer profits, often quite
unconsciously, from the efforts of the masters who have
preceded him. In a *Partisan Review* symposium in 1939
Anderson was asked whether as a writer he was aware
of a "usable past." His answer was a self-portrait in mini-
ature: "I am afraid I do not know what you mean by
'usable past.' . . . I am afraid that my difficulty in trying to answer these questions is that I spend little time
thinking of either past or future. It is my passionate desire to live in the NOW. Mine is not a critical mind."
And even when he did acknowledge a relationship to the
past, it was usually to cite an heroic writer's resistance
against society rather than to comment on a complication
of thought, an enrichment of theme, a mastery of language. As Lionel Trilling has remarked, "His awareness
of the past was limited, perhaps by his fighting faith in

the 'modern,' and this, in a modern, is always a danger"
—particularly, one might add, when it is the dubious
modern of the "Chicago Renaissance."

In the ingenuousness with which he articulated his
creed of the artist as a folk-inspired amateur and in the insistence with which he rehearsed, through a variety of
symbolic guises, his liberation from the bourgeois world,
Anderson made of his life a culture-legend which often
overshadowed his work. This legend soon became a
model of the struggle for articulation—or rather the struggle for identity through a cathartic articulation—in which
so many untutored but gifted young American writers invariably engaged. Just as Anderson always found it necessary to erect elaborate barriers against the world from
which he had escaped in 1912, so they wrote to purge
themselves, again and again, of its corruptions, its bar-
barisms, and its constrictions. That world, however, was
not easily shaken off and it showed its ultimate power
over American writers in their compulsive need to ex-
pend a high proportion of their energy in denying it.
For Anderson and for others like him, writing was at
least as much a means by which to forge a personal identity as it was an objective discipline of the imagination.
No wonder so many of the writers who came after Anderson, both Thomas Wolfe the individual and the innumerable facsimile Thomas Wolfes, recognized in their
lives one or another variant of his legend. Anderson
seemed the archetype of all those writers who were trying to raise themselves to art by sheer emotion and sheer
will, who suspected intellect as a cosmopolitan snare that
would destroy their gift for divining America's mystic
essence, and who abominated the society which had

formed them but knew no counterpoise of value by which to escape its moral dominion.

It is in terms of his legend, and the needs which impelled him to advance it, that we can best understand Anderson's literary stances and stratagems. Consider, for one, his persistent assumption of innocence or what, in another context, has been called the credo of defenselessness: that literary approach to complex situations and ideas which insists on discounting their complexity in the name of creative passion. After a time, no doubt, Anderson did exploit his innocence, perhaps because he sensed that there are situations in which defenselessness frankly acknowledged is the only possible defense. But can one doubt that his stance of innocence was originally an authentic response to a cultural situation he could not cope with, a situation which led him to elaborate his personal legend of the Liberated Artist? Or consider, again, the vague mysticism which creeps into some, though not the best, of his work. No doubt, after a while he turned to it in laziness, using a gaseous filler to occupy the vacuum left by failures of his imagination. But can one doubt that at one time his mysticism was a genuine reflection of the artist's awe before the disordered multiplicity of outer things and inner relations?

Between the legend he made for himself and the pattern of deprivation which weaves through his life there was, of course, a tie of complex interdependence. Without the deprivation there would have been no need for the legend, and without the legend no way to overcome— or evade—the deprivation. In one strand of his work, the lesser strand, legend and deprivation can be seen reinforcing each other. This is the Anderson of the political mindlessness of *Marching Men,* the emasculated sexuality of *Many Marriages,* the folk clichés of *Dark Laughter;* the Anderson who took to cultural fashion the way other novelists take to drink; who staked everything on enthusiasm and sentiment and in their absence tried awkwardly to simulate them; who saw the artist's life as an unambiguous struggle of defiant rectitude against commercial contamination; who was forever concerned with a search for freedom but lacked the spiritual rigor to define that freedom in terms of the scope and tension it had had for the great writers of the past. And this, finally, is the Anderson of whom Lionel Trilling's severe characterization is, alas, true: the Anderson whose "affirmation of life by love, passion and freedom had, paradoxically enough, the effect of quite negating life, making it grey, empty, and devoid of meaning. We are quite used to hearing that this is what excessive intellection can do; we are not so often warned that emotion . . . can be similarly destructive."

In one sentence of a letter he wrote to his brother Karl in 1931, this Anderson reached his most complete and succinct self-expression: "I hardly know what I can teach except anti-success." His whole literary life had been a long, gnarled yet not unheroic struggle to teach "anti-success"; but though it would never cease to be indispensable, this teaching was never quite enough, if only because in Anderson's over-simple terms it could not provide a sufficiently resilient barrier to the world of "success."

There are critics and readers for whom this is the *only* Anderson. They acknowledge the pathos and sincerity of his effort but see it merely as another instance of the incompleteness and truncation so pervasive in American culture. This is a view which becomes virtually mandatory once Anderson is considered in the terms he himself occasionally proposed: as a prophet and visionary. Read for moral explication, as a guide to life, his work must seem unsatisfactory; it simply does not tell us enough. But there is another, more fruitful way of reading his work: as the expression of a sensitive witness to the national experience and as the achievement of a story teller who created a small body of fiction unique in American writing for the lyrical purity of its feeling. So regarded, his best work becomes a durable part of the American literary structure.

Unquestionably durable is Anderson's testimony on the most dramatic social development in American life, the transition from an agrarian to an industrial society. No novelist, no historian has portrayed this segment of American experience with an intimacy and poignancy superior to Anderson's in *Poor White* and in his stories; no other American writer has so thoroughly communicated the sense of that historical moment when the native sweetness had not yet been lost to our life, when the nation fumbled on the verge of outwardness and began to stir from provinciality but had not yet toughened into imperial assurance. In the shabby crevices of this world Anderson discovered the lonely and deformed souls who would never be noticed by official society. In the craftsmen of the towns, whom history had passed by and left stricken and helpless, he found concealed reserves of feeling, of muted torment and love. More than most of his contemporaries among American writers, Anderson insisted that frustration and deprivation were at the base of American life, but he did so in order to credit the unused emotional resources, the unmeasured potentials that were also there. For years he bore a literary grudge against Sinclair Lewis because he suspected that beneath the brilliance of satire Lewis was selling his people short.

Anderson's America was not the powerhouse of willful myth-makers, not a sounding-board for autoerotic effusions, not even the air-conditioned nightmare of fashionable rejection—it was a social memory uniquely tender and vulnerable. This was an America to which even the most disaffected of urban intellectuals could admit an allegiance, an America not yet committed to power and accumulation. That Anderson's critique of capitalism from the standpoint of craftsmanship soon seemed naïve and inadequate hardly mattered; what evoked one's affection was the feeling behind that critique, a feeling perhaps available to all conditions of society but most deeply rooted in that epoch of American life which, at least in retrospect, suggests something of the quality of adolescence.

It is precisely this quality of adolescence, whether taken as an independent emotional datum or as a reflection of an historical moment, which has caused most of the uncertainties and difficulties in our response to Anderson's work. Though the depiction of adolescent traumas is a recurrent theme in American literature, adolescence itself is an area of experience towards which Americans remain conspicuously uneasy. They suspect, even as they remember with yearning, its flow of unsorted emotion. In their commitment to an ethos of visible achievement and status, they fear the tenderness of adolescence as an emotion which may deflect them from their ambitions or expose them to the world's ridicule. And those of us who resist this dominant ethos often find that the constricting role of resistance is itself a block to affective largesse. The height of American wisdom is to search for something called maturity—and it is the prevalence of this search in our national life which most definitively indicates the absence of genuine maturity.

With such conditioning attitudes, we must necessarily respond in terms of bedeviled ambiguity to a writer like Anderson. Almost always we categorize him as a writer who moved us greatly in adolescence but now lacks the power to affect us in maturity—as if it were quite safe to assume that our adolescent responses were so patently invalid and unworthy of selective preservation, or as if we could safely compartmentalize our lives, simply discarding in adulthood what we were in our youth. When we use the tag of adolescence to dismiss Anderson's work we forget that even in our first reading his stories appealed to our sense of "oldness" rather than immaturity, that often enough it was in those stories that we were first touched by forebodings of decay and loss. By falsely reducing adolescence to the merely callow and sentimental, we evade the real problem posed by Anderson's work, which is to discriminate between feeling realized and feeling forced or simulated. And when we say—this is the favorite gambit of hostile critics—that Anderson's work deals not with reality but with adolescent gropings, we ignore the reality of those very gropings; we ignore, as well, the fact that from these gropings none of us is or should be exempt. Alfred Kazin has put this matter well:

When we think of the many who have written more sharply than [Anderson], who have not been content to rest on the expression of dismay, the air of grief, we tend to grow dubious about his significance. What has he done but prepare isolated histories of the puzzled and the bewildered? Perhaps they are not enough, but it is also true that there has always been something of ourselves that we have seen in them, some moment in our lives that was illuminated by theirs.

The gropings in Anderson's work are never in themselves to be condemned. Anderson himself once wrote a chilling rebuke to those who so dismiss him: "I don't think it matters much, all this calling a man muddler, groper etc. . . . the very man who throws such words as these knows in his heart that he is also facing a wall." Anderson's work becomes objectionable only when he ceases to grope, ceases to extend his curiosity and affection; only when he begins to imitate and unwittingly caricature the eagerness and openness of his best writing. The critic's job then becomes one of discriminating between that part of Anderson's work in which callowness and sentimentality frequently corrupt his achievement and that more durable part in which adolescence comes through in a radiant comeliness, a sweet surge of affectivity. Once such a distinction is made there can be no question about the value of *Winesburg* and *Poor White*, of "Death in the Woods" and "The Man Who Became a Woman."

It now becomes possible to consider the question that must suggest itself to every student of Anderson's career: what should he have done after his brief burst of fertility, after *Winesburg* and *The Triumph of the Egg?* The critical point of his career came at about 1923, the year when both *Horses and Men* and *Many Marriages* were published. *Horses and Men* was the last sustained expression of his most successful native manner, and *Many Marriages* the beginning of his disastrous venture into Lawrencian precincts. Among Anderson's friends and critics there have been two opinions about the crisis he then faced. For his Chicago friends and a few of his critics Anderson was essentially a folk or sectional writer who did his best work in the Midwest and was bewildered and contaminated by the cosmopolitan East. For his New York friends and most of his critics Anderson was a writer of undisciplined talent who, after a few creative years, desperately needed a sustaining vision of life and an organized knowledge of craft.

Abstractly, either of these estimates of Anderson, if they led to a consistent course of action, might have helped him avoid his debacles. Had he deliberately restricted himself to the short forms in which his talent was most at home, to those subjects he knew surpassingly well, and to a program of selective and sparse publication, he might have continued producing first-rate stories in the *Winesburg* manner. Had he made a herculean effort to educate himself to the complexities of modern life and thought, to use his mind at its full potential, and to relate himself actively to the great tradition of the novel, he might just possibly have become an interesting social novelist. But in actuality neither of these choices was available to him.

Anderson's Chicago friends ignore the fact that he was "contaminated" by cosmopolitanism before he left the Midwest; the whole bent of his literary life was toward the big city, toward the aggressively modern. He could not retreat to some memory of the past or region of the present because both memory and region were in process of dissolution; in modern America there was not even the marginal place for Anderson's Ohio that there was for Faulkner's Mississippi. Had he persisted in the *Winesburg* manner he might have left a greater body of successful work than he actually did, but the fact is that all the pressures of both his environment and his own ambition drove him to abandon that manner.

Still less practical was the other proposed course. By 1923 Anderson was a man in his late forties who had gone through the most painful struggles merely to become a writer and had at last won praise to an extent he could hardly have anticipated. The kind of transformation which might have made him a highly conscious artist would have been possible only under the urging and guidance of an authoritative body of literary opinion. But it was precisely this opinion which was missing from American life: the culture of the 1920's was itself beset by the weaknesses that would soon cripple Anderson. (Scott Fitzgerald, for example, wrote that *Many Marriages* was Anderson's best book!) To have urged, in these circumstances, that Anderson attempt a total self-transformation would merely have been an oblique way of suggesting that he stop writing. It was his tragedy that after the early 1920's he was trapped between two worlds: he could find sustenance neither in the deep kinships of the folk bard nor in the demanding traditions of the sophisticated artist.

If, for the biographer, Anderson's career must seem a dramatic instance of a gifted writer impoverished by a constricting culture, the critic can rest his final attention on that small segment of Anderson's work in which he overcame those constrictions. Precious as it would be at any time, that segment assumes a particular value in our present cultural situation.

There is a sense in which it may be said that Anderson has not had an appreciable influence on American writing. To be sure, there are Steinbeck and Saroyan who have brought to extremity the inferior aspects of his work. And there is Hemingway who repudiated Anderson in the name of craft but still owes him many debts. But while Steinbeck and Saroyan could enlarge on his occasional sentimentalism and Hemingway could tighten and rigidify his style, no American writer has yet been able to realize that strain of lyrical and nostalgic feeling which in Anderson's best work reminds one of another and greater poet of tenderness, Turgeniev. At his best Anderson creates a world of authentic sentiment, and while part of the meaning of his career is that sentiment is not enough for a writer, the careers of those who follow him —those who swerve to Steinbeck's sentimentality or Hemingway's toughness—illustrate how rare genuine sentiment still is in our literature.

During the last two decades our dominant writing has been shaped by the Hemingway manner. Our literature has been characterized by crude and violent action, speech distorted into stylized bravado, an aggressive scorn of the mind, and a fearful retreat from direct emotion. Too often it has seemed a mere reflection of the tendency in modern society to see life stripped of emotional inwardness, and men as mere objects. That this vision is often expressed with great skill is also characteristic of a culture which can do the most wretched things in the most efficient way.

By comparison Anderson's work must seem almost anachronistic, for no one can deny that our present world is closer to Hemingway than to Anderson. What can we make of a writer in whom there sometimes still runs freely and sweetly an affection for all things sentient?

But surely there is, there should be a place in our culture, even if only a minor one, for Sherwood Anderson. His faults, his failures and defeats can hardly be ignored: he was almost always limited in moral sensibility and social perspective. Yet there were a few moments when he spoke, as almost no one else among American writers, with the voice of love.

Bibliographical Note

BIBLIOGRAPHY

An incomplete bibliographical listing is in Fred B. Millett's *Contemporary American Authors*. A fuller though still not complete listing, by Raymond Gozzi, appears in *The Newberry Library Bulletin*, December 1948.

WORKS

There is no collected edition of Anderson's works. Since his death two generous anthologies have appeared: *The Anderson Reader* edited by Paul Rosenfeld and *The Anderson Portable* edited by Horace Gregory. *Winesburg, Ohio* is in the Modern Library and has also been reprinted in a paper-covered pocket edition.

BIOGRAPHY

No full-scale biography of Anderson has yet appeared. *Story* magazine, September-October 1941, contains indis-

pensable memoirs by close friends: Paul Rosenfeld, Lewis
Galantière, James Boyd, Marsden Hartley, and Harry
Hansen. *The Newberry Library Bulletin,* December
1948, has equally valuable recollections by George Daugherty, Waldo Frank, and Roger Sergel. Edmund Wilson's
anthology, *The Shock of Recognition,* offers a selection of
Anderson's letters to Van Wyck Brooks, and *Paul Rosenfeld, Voyager in the Arts,* edited by Jerome Mellquist
and Lucie Wiese, contains a selection of Anderson's letters to Rosenfeld. Some of the most penetrating remarks ever made about Anderson appear in Gertrude
Stein's *The Autobiography of Alice B. Toklas.*

An anonymous recollection of Anderson as an advertising man appears in *Advertising and Selling,* December
17, 1936. "My Brother, Sherwood Anderson," an article by
Karl Anderson in *The Saturday Review of Literature,*
September 4, 1948, is important but has many errors.
Sherwood Anderson's Formative Years, an unpublished
dissertation by William Sutton (Ohio State University,
1943), is a painstaking and reliable reconstruction of Anderson's life until 1912. *Sherwood Anderson's Winesburg, Ohio,* an unpublished dissertation by William Phillips (University of Chicago, 1949) has much useful material and comment on the early years.

Many books have been published which contain reminiscences of the "Chicago Renaissance" and Anderson's role
in it: *My Thirty Years' War* by Margaret Anderson, *Mid-
Western Portraits* by Harry Hansen, *Troubadour* by Alfred Kreymborg, *The World at My Shoulder* by Eunice
Tietjens, *A Poet's Life* by Harriet Monroe.

Indispensable to any student is the collection of Anderson correspondence and manuscripts in The Newberry Library, Chicago.

CRITICISM

The best single piece of criticism on Anderson, unsurpassed in sympathy and acuity, is Waldo Frank's brief essay on *Winesburg* in *Story*, September-October 1941. Of the two early books written on Anderson, Cleveland Chase's *Sherwood Anderson* is mildly depreciatory and Byrillion Fagin's *The Phenomenon of Sherwood Anderson* wildly ecstatic. Both the attack and the defense have been superseded by recent critical pieces: Lionel Trilling's "Sherwood Anderson" in *Kenyon Review*, Summer 1941 (also in his book, *The Liberal Imagination*), a powerful and cogent statement of the view that Anderson is ultimately an unsatisfactory writer, and Horace Gregory's introduction to *The Portable Anderson*, a temperate and persuasive statement of the favorable view. Maxwell Geismar's essay on Anderson in *The Last of the Provincials* is extremely sympathetic but often undiscriminating. There are valuable observations on Anderson in Alfred Kazin's *On Native Grounds* and Oscar Cargill's *Intellectual America*. Frederick Hoffman's *Freudianism and the Literary Mind* has a useful chapter on Anderson and the Freudianism of the 1920's, which would be still more useful if it considered Lawrence as an influence on Anderson. Thomas Whipple's essay on Anderson in *Spokesman* is a good piece of sociological criticism. And Wyndham Lewis's attack in *Paleface* is important historically though unacceptable as criticism.

Readers interested in the shifts of critical attitude toward Anderson might consult the following books: Paul Rosenfeld's *Port of New York*, Rebecca West's *The Strange Necessity*, John McCole's *Lucifer at Large*, V. F. Calverton's *The Newer Spirit*, and Granville Hicks's *The Great Tradition*.

ADDENDUM, 1966

Two notable contributions to the study of Anderson have been published since 1951: *Letters of Sherwood Anderson*, edited by Howard Mumford Jones and Walter B. Rideout (1953), and *Sherwood Anderson: Short Stories*, edited by Maxwell Geismar (1962).

The most recent critical work is Rex Burbank's *Sherwood Anderson* (1964).

Indexes

General Index

Index

O'Hara, *Butterfield 8*, 233
Oppenheim, James, 113

Paden, Cliff, (John Emerson)
    and Jeanette, 28, 133
Partisan Review, 245
Pater, Walter, 70-71
Perkins, Maxwell, 235, 237
Phelps, William Lyon, 58
Poetry, 59, 70, 75
Populism, 61, 87-88
Post-Impressionist painters, 59
Pound, Ezra, 59, 60, 75
Prall, Elizabeth, *see* Anderson,
    Mrs. Sherwood (3)
Proust, Marcel, 152
psychoanalysis, 69, 179-81

radicalism, 219-24
Rascoe, Burton, 67, 74, 75, 239
Reader, 36
Ripshin, 205-206
Rolland, *Jean-Christophe*, 58
Rorty, James, 219
Rosenfeld, Paul, 114, 118, 119,
    120-21, 122, 131, 132, 136,
    181, 199, 209, 221-22

Sandburg, Carl, 59, 60, 61
Saroyan, William, 237-38, 255
Saturday Evening Post, 144
*Saturday Review of Litera-
ture*, 135
Schevill, Ferdinand, 143, 213,
    239
Scribner's, 221

Sergel, Roger, 241
Seven Arts, 106, 113, 114
Simmons, Harry, 32
Smith, Emma, *see* Anderson,
    Mrs. Irwin
Smith, Mrs. (SA's grand-
    mother), 11
Smyth County News, 206
Socialism, 61, 69, 219
Spanish-American War, 28-29
Springfield Republic-Times,
    32
Stalin, Josef, 222, 224
Stedman, Edmund Clarence,
    57
Stein, Gertrude, 95-96, 132-33,
    142, 200, 202, 208, 239
    *Autobiography of Alice B.
    Toklas*, 132, 202
    Geography and Plays, 133
    Tender Buttons, 95
    Three Lives, 96
Steinbeck, John, 255
Stieglitz, Alfred, 197, 200, 239
Stone & Kimball, 57
strikes, *see* labor unions
Sutton, William, 14, 43

Taylor-Critchfield agency, 51,
    53, 55, 119
Terry, Florence, 45
Theatre Guild, 238
Tietjens, Eunice, 62, 70, 75
Tolstoy, *The Death of Ivan
    Ilytch*, 166
Trilling, Lionel, 217, 245, 248
Trotsky, Leon, 137

Index of Works